Never Better

essays

Danielle Oubeck

ISBN 978-1-66788-888-0

This book is dedicated to you and me.

For getting through 100% of our worst days.

"Grief. The pain now is part of the happiness then. That's the deal."

-CS Lewis

Contents

ONE

I'm Glad You're Here

Welcome to my nightmare!

We have endless reflections on life, death, and being left behind, and we snack in the middle of the night. If you've found yourself here because you lost your person, I am sorry. You only know the horror when it happens to you. There aren't enough words in the world to convey the misery of missing someone who has passed, and I don't wish it on anyone. The unfortunate deal with life is that no matter what, we either die young or live long enough to grieve our loved ones.

This book is not for everyone. Sarcasm is the best way for me to cope, and if you're like me, sometimes laughing helps ease the pain of loss and life. Much of what I write about is not inherently funny - trauma, miscarriages, eating disorders - none of those acts as a springboard into a fit of laughter. How I have dealt with the unfortunate sides of

1

life we've all experienced is with a sarcastic remark that sometimes makes me feel quite a bit better and makes others slightly uncomfortable. I'm David punching up at the Goliath that is the universe. I would never make light of someone else's grief, trauma, or bad day. But my own? Girl...

Grief is isolating and terrifying, but the phenomenal thing about it is the universality of the whole production. We labor into life, every single one of us, and then – we labor out. We watch those around us live and breathe, and then die. Leaving business unresolved. Leaving a pile of chaotic sadness in their wake. What I have searched for in my own sorrow is a connection and an understanding that, while devastating, it is an event we will all eventually know intimately. The tricky part comes when it is all out of the natural order we've come to expect of our world. When we lose our spouse at 33. When we lose a child, a pregnancy, a sibling. When we lose ourselves.

My loss is not unique. People die every day. This is not the grief Olympics. But the pain and isolation I have experienced was unique to me. It made me search for some kind of understanding that maybe putting up walls to keep the bad parts of life out is a futile waste of time. The bad will always find its way in because life is poorly insulated. We must be vulnerable to search for the good.

I'm thankful for the advent of websites that tell you if a dog is hurt or dies in a movie so that I know not to watch it. I need that trigger warning. And so, I am offering the following trigger warning to you, dear reader. I do write about my experience of suicide ideation. If this is not the book for you, please join me in my next one where I hope to be more mentally well, and the topics will lean more toward my devout defense for Arby's being the superior fast-food chain.

This book is dedicated to and for:

— Fellow widows and survivors of life

— LGBTQAI+ community and allies

— Bernie Sanders

— Those who have done our country a service and worked in retail/food/healthcare

— Anyone who is unashamed of their passion, talent, and creativity

— People who talk to dogs before they address the human

— Imposter syndrome sufferers

— Those who say "I should be heading out" before a host must awkwardly think of an excuse to get you to leave

— Empaths

— Parents & those in the struggle

— People who share memes on social media

— Those who are bad at math

— Those who are good at math but who remain
  humble about it

— People who know a little too much about true
  crime as a hobby

— and Muggsy Bogues, the shortest player to ever
  play in the NBA

TWO

Losing Andrew

It's Thursday, and the March rain outside is cool and drizzling. My husband pads into the bedroom quietly, as I squeeze my eyes shut, holding onto the predawn darkness before I'd go into the hospital and tackle the ramped-up beginnings of the pandemic. He would go into work, the same as he did every morning before that for the last ten years. A steel factory in Detroit that became like his second home. He leans down to kiss me on the forehead.

"I love you," he whispers quietly.

Watching through half-opened eyes as he walks out of the room, my last image of him alive burns into my mind. His black beanie cap around his head. This work shirt, sleeves rolled up, would be shoved into his jacket labeled "Andrew".

I love you. The last thing I'd ever hear him say. I couldn't wake myself up enough to say it back. He knows I love him, I thought. Saying I love you when you've been together for ten years becomes perfunctory – not much genuine passion behind words that held your life together.

Consumed with work on the designated Covid unit, and still blissfully unaware of how bad things were about to get, the nursing team was still determining how we would take on the pandemic. Barely having a moment to look at my phone, I texted him.

2:24 pm: "Ugh, I'm working on the unit where all of the Covid patients are."

2:26 pm: "Why? Didn't you just get pulled to work there?"

I returned the phone to my pocket and went back to the nurses' station to get my new patient assignment. By 2:43 pm, I had ten missed calls and a message from an unknown number - "This is Andrew's work. He's had an accident. Please call me".

Awesome, I thought to myself. Just what we needed. He had cut himself with steel or worse; he lost an arm. Now I'm going to have to do everything myself. Now I'm married to the one-armed guy. The selfish annoyance made me shake my head. I quickly cycled through the index of injuries he had previously sustained from working at a steel factory and decided it couldn't be anything too bad. That doesn't happen, right? A person doesn't die at work. A person doesn't die at 36. He had just texted me; he must be fine.

A minute later I was on the phone with his work. "Andrew has had an accident. The ambulance is here and taking him to the hospital," terror struck me. Why wasn't he the one calling me? Surely if it was serious, he would be the one to call.

"Is he okay?" I asked with bated breath. My last millisecond before the floor would fall out from underneath me and I would die too. The last breath before our lives crumbled and something insidious took its place.

I took inventory of everything around me. The scattering of busy nurses came to a hush as all eyes fell on me. The sterile hospital smell consumed me, and I felt a rush of nausea. The floor, gleaming with a shine from a waxing a few hours before. The Sharpie pen I twisted between my fingers. The click of the cap against my thumb.

"They were able to get a pulse back," she stammered.

That was it. Those words swept out the last bit of energy I had in my body, and I fell to the floor. My fingertips braced my body as I fell forward. I'm going to puke. Arms circled me and led me to a chair.

7

"You have to breathe!"

"What happened? Are you okay?"

A group gathered around me. What could possibly be going on within our nightmare we were all already living, my coworkers wondered.

"I think my husband is dead," I said as I stared at the bulletin board in front of me. Colorful paper surrounded by safety metrics, reminders to keep everyone safe. And then, I let out a cry. The shriek of a mortally wounded animal.

Somehow, I found myself at the hospital where he was taken – in the passenger seat of a car driven by a coworker I had just met that morning. "I can talk or not talk. You tell me what you need," she said, as she reached over and grabbed my hand.

I stood awkwardly at the security desk in the empty emergency room lobby. Shifting from one foot to another, the sweat trickled down my back. Covid had cleared the hospital waiting room out, aside from a nervous wife who was about to become a widow.

"Mrs. Oubeck?" A nurse, a fellow soldier in the war of an unknown virus, walked me into a small room with three chairs. The energy and the sadness that hung in the air told me that this room was for bad news. "The doctor will be here in a moment".

This room of sadness and death couldn't possibly be for me. This was for secondhand stories you hear about or in movies. You don't find yourself in this situation.

"Why won't they just take me to him?" I grabbed a tissue, as my coworker stood next to me, a sturdy pillar of support. This morning she was going in for a busy shift. Eight hours later she was at another hospital and holding together a stranger on the worst day of her life. "Thursdays, am I right?" I looked up at her. My last bit of humor was given to her as a thank you for being in the bad news room with me.

"Mrs. Oubeck, your husband had an accident at work," the doctor stepped into the room. All business, no remorse. That is how we handle things, but this is different. This is my tragedy. I am on the other side of hell. "We did everything we could…"

The air sucked out of the room, and a guttural cry echoed through the halls. A thrash, "don't say it, please don't say it." Screaming. Why is it so loud? Who is carrying on so much? The sounds are coming from me. I fall out of the chair, ready to vomit.

"But he did not survive his injuries. I'm sorry for your loss."

Sedate me. Please, sedate me. Or wake me up from this nightmare.

"No. No. This is not right. You have the wrong person. You didn't do everything you could. Let me see him! This is some kind of mistake."

If I repeat it enough, the nightmare before me would fade away. I would open my eyes and see him leaving for work that morning. I'd muster up enough energy to say 'I love you' back to him. I'd learn my lesson the same way Dickens wanted Ebenezer to be reformed. I was bargaining with anyone who would listen.

My mom arrived just in time for us to be taken back to see him. We stood before the trauma bay doors, and I stopped. It reminded me of our wedding. On a miserably hot day in July, light oak double doors in front of me – ready to be opened and presented to my husband. I'd walk down the aisle and we'd begin our lives together. The doors were prettier in the chapel.

"I need a second," I took a deep breath. I wasn't sure how I would survive seeing him.

Another breath, and then a step forward. I'm looking at the floors, freshly waxed just like the ones at my work. This one was littered with gloves and packages of medication. Signs of a futile battle lost.

He lay alone in the middle of a bay. A frigid hospital. He must be cold, I thought. The endotracheal tube protruding the side of his mouth, his beautiful half-opened eye – lifeless and unresponsive.

Some kind of horrific stare that makes you question what awaits us on the other side.

I fell onto his chest. No. No. No.

"Take a breath. You have to breathe," the nurse yells at me, as I yell at him. Breathe.

The defibrillation pads are still on his chest. Blunt force trauma to the head. A towel circled around him, ear to ear, to avoid seeing the worst of it. I held his hand, still slightly warm, but discolored. The signs of death I was familiar with, on a man I was familiar with. It was not real.

"Come back to me, please come back to me," I begged him, God, the universe, whoever would answer me to undo this wrong. But it was real. Life was drained out of him, and thus me.

There were phone calls and papers signed, a blur of chaos. All I could think of was how he'd be alone. I didn't want to leave him there by himself.

I left the hospital with a small bag of the few things he had on him. The remnants of a life – a father, a husband, a friend. Someone obsessed with HGTV. Someone who was supposed to come home that night and play UNO with his daughter.

We stepped outside into the drizzly afternoon. What do I even do now? Our six-year-old, KG, was in the parking garage with her grandpa. Unaware of how her life was forever altered. Blissful, naive to death and sadness, as a child should remain. Six years with her dad is all she would get. I would be the messenger to deliver her the news.

I curled her into my arms and sat on the ground. Cradling her head, her little hands, her eyes that were her father's brimming with tears and confusion.

"How can daddy be gone? It's almost his birthday," I rocked her back and forth, sitting on the cold cement, no answers for either of us.

The worst was yet to come. The sleepless nights, anxiety, and grief were only beginning. Our old life was over.

THREE

Cremation

It's mid evening, and my mom is helping KG wash her hair in the bathroom across from my bedroom. The doors are open and I'm listening as she sings the wrong words to Starman by David Bowie, which is her obsession at the moment. I need the help of parenting duties because it's taking every bit of energy I have to just be alive these days. We're in the nucleus of our tragedy. I'm kneeling on the hardwood in front of Andrew's closet, like a sacred altar. I need to pick an outfit to cremate him in.

Cremation. Even the word sounds like an assault. Why can't I live in a society with a better relationship with death and dying? I want to bring him home, celebrate his life. Put baked goods on his grave every Día de Muertos. I want to bury him with everything he's ever loved to take with him to the other side. I want to bury him with me.

My mind scans every bit of trauma and grief I'd ever second hand-edly experienced, read or watched on a film. How do other people handle these chaotic life changing moments? I need someone to tell me what to do next, how to fix this mistake, how to exist in a world where my husband's cerebellum is "pulpified" as the medical examiner noted. The song To Build a Home by the Cinematic Orchestra plays over and over in my head, and I wonder if this is hell. Maybe it is me who has died, and I am living in purgatory.

I was too flippant, I thought to myself as I took his favorite sweatshirt off a hanger and pulled it over my head. I was aware that I didn't fully deserve any of the good things the universe gave me: a wonderful husband, a healthy and beautiful child, the life of my dreams. Maybe if I keep quiet, the universe wouldn't notice it had made a mistake. I was grateful, thankful, blessed – all of the Hobby Lobby signs, but it caught up to me. The universe caught up and took it away.

There's a black plastic bin of his shoes in his closet - Chuck Taylor Converse of every color - and I collapse over them. Protecting them from the fall out of the bomb that exploded our lives. I breathe in his smell. Deep hints of his peppermint beard oil and his stinky shoes. He was so particular with his clothes. Before I know what I'm doing, I climb into the bin with the shoes. I'm crying, gathering them in my arms.

"Is mama ok?" KG is out of the shower and peering into the room, hair dripping wet onto the floors Andrew had just refinished a few months prior. She's wrapped in a towel and then up into my mother's arms - up and away from the sad scene before them. I'm causing her more trauma to see me falling apart, I think. I must get up and do better, but I cannot leave this bin of his shoes. The shoes that his feet will never slide into again.

I compose myself enough to stand and stare at his shirts. Button down plaid shirts he wore religiously. I gather them in a hug and fall forward. Maybe he's still in there under all the cotton thread. Maybe there's a link to him here. Deep, deep in my lungs I breathe him in. Acqua di Gio and Tide. The smell of him is a mixture of the steel industry that he could never completely scrub off him and sandal-wood. It's all there, tied up in clothes he'd never wear again. A shirt with a tag still on it for a vacation we'd never go on.

I picked a blue button-down shirt - nothing fancy - but one he wore all the time and was his favorite. His blue socks with whales on them. Oh, the socks! He was crazy about his obnoxious patterned socks. His Detroit baseball cap he rarely went without. It smelt of his peppermint shampoo. A different hat he wore to work that day - the one which couldn't stop the machine from crushing his head - was still in a hospital bag on my nightstand. What do you do with the souvenirs of death?

I'm torn. I don't want to take his favorite things in to be cremated. I don't want him to be cremated. Taken from us and turned to ash. I want to bring him home. The thought of him lying in a cold cooler, the sterile smell of medicine and death circling him was enough to stop my heart. He was there, and here I am. Helpless to do anything but bundle up clothes that smell of him and cry.

FOUR

The Wake

I don't remember much from the immediate aftermath of Andrew dying. I blamed part of the memory loss on covid, and then began to suspect it was from the Lexapro I was newly prescribed. It wasn't until I was months out did I realize that widow brain fog was a thing. What I do remember is that my days were filled with awkward interactions orchestrated entirely by me.

The day after he passed, I had to go to the medical examiner to identify him. My sister Kris and I piled into Andrew's car to pick up my friend Kelly to go downtown. We had just pulled out of our driveway when I saw my neighbor and her daughters playing outside. Until this point, we had only had two or three conversations – one of which was about a recent miscarriage I had suffered. If there was ever an Eeyore in the Hundred Acre Woods of our cul-de-sac, it was me. I'm the spritely lady who was always showing up in sweatpants with bad news.

"Stop for a second," I told my sister, and I jumped out of the car with a quickness that scared both Kris and my neighbor.

"Go inside girls," she motioned for the kids to run for the porch from the weirdo who just bailed out of a moving vehicle in front of their home.

"Hey, I just wanted to tell you, um, I'll be having people over. It's not because I don't believe covid is real. It's because Andrew died."

"Oh my god, I am so sorry. Who?" She raised her hands to her mouth with both sympathy and confusion. I realized she probably didn't know who I was talking about. It could have been one of the thousands of dogs we had shacked up at the house for all she knew.

"Andrew, my husband. His name is Andrew. He's dead," I was in Andrew's sweatshirt and pants, and standing there in shock. Just blabbering on and trauma dumping on everyone in my path. We were relatively new to the neighborhood, and there we were. The Oubeck family – some of us dead and the live ones were crazy.

"Oh my god, I am so sorry." She shook her head in disbelief. She reached her arm out, to start to embrace me, and we both backed a few feet away. Covid was a real dark cloud reminding us to keep to ourselves.

"I know. Yeah, it's bad," I shouted from across the driveway. "There was an accident at work. I'm going to see him now. His body, I mean. I just wanted you to know why there are cars over if you see them," I motioned towards my house. It looked smaller from across the street. I tried to remember the day we looked at the house to buy it. It wasn't yet two years before Andrew died that we decided to purchase the house, and it would be our forever home.

If you're reading this over my shoulder as a ghost, Andrew, I want you to know that dying during the beginning of a pandemic was a dick move. I could barely see him in the hospital. The medical examiner made Kelly stand outside in the freezing rain, while Kristen and I stood in a sad conference type room that smelled like blue cheese.

"His picture will come on the screen right there," the lady at the office motioned to a small TV. "I'll give you a few minutes."

And as she promised, there he was. That's him. The worst sight to ever behold – your person's dead face on a 14-inch Samsung. If I close my eyes now, I can still see his face in that moment. Him, but not him at all. Whatever makes a person a person, was gone.

I signed some papers and was shoved out of the office so that the workers could get back to whatever they were cooking with blue cheese. Then it was off to the funeral home to continue our morbid tour of death. The funeral director sat across the room from us, giving us the spiel of what our options were. "Do you know what he would have wanted?"

"Probably not to die," I thought. I went through an entire box of tissues as I listened to them tell me a funeral wasn't really an option because of covid restrictions. Why do all funeral homes have the same vibe? I mean, I know it's because people are dead, and we are mourning them. But can they at least try for any other aroma than floral and 90s trauma?

I hosted a small wake at our home. Someone organized food and my family cleaned my house, but I don't remember the logistics. It's all snapshots. It's a vision of me lying in bed staring at his photos, and the next thing I know, there are people in my house telling me how sorry they are.

Friends who I hadn't made time to see in forever showed up and witnessed my pain. "Covid wouldn't keep us away," they said, as they embraced me. Andrew's coworkers came and got to see the other side of his life. His PlayStation controllers were still laying out on the table, his coffee mug, the dining room table he had just purchased.

A few weeks before he passed, Kelly and I were out for brunch with our friend Maddie.

"Want to go get our noses pierced?" We casually discussed over a Bloody Mary and French toast. We found a place down the street and headed there as I made a quick call to Andrew.

"I know I'm 33, but will you still love me if I get my nose pierced?" I needed expressed permission and confirmation that he would still in fact love me.

"Are you serious? I don't care," I could hear him rolling his eyes through the phone. After ten years, he was used to my impetuous nature and learned to roll with the punches. He had to deal with a peppering of questioning like "Would you still love me if I were a worm?" and "What if I was just a torso, would our relationship change?" It was the mental illness and overthinking of it all…

I made the impulsive decision to change my post nose piercing to a hoop the day of Andrew's wake. I couldn't control much in my life, and I don't remember most of the day, but I do remember consciously looking in the mirror and saying, "today's the day we change this piercing".

A few hours into the ordeal, my nose started to swell from changing it too early. I took out the hoop and couldn't figure out the corkscrew post to get it back into my nose. I started crying and texted Kelly, "I need you upstairs, emergency". She was in the bathroom two seconds later, a look of sympathy on her face. What a pitiful sight. My hair unbrushed, my face red with frustration and terror, sweaty with a swollen nose.

"I can't get this fuckin thing back in," I cried.

She got the post back in. I returned to the wake and had everyone leave. I thought it would be helpful to be surrounded by others who loved Andrew and loved me, but it felt suffocating worrying about other's grief. They left and I stood in our empty living room, asking to only myself and Andrew's ghost, "now what?"

FIVE

PhD in Mediocrity

I'm suffering from an affliction, and it's one that many people are plagued with. Most people I know who are ailed come to grips with it. They learn to live a normal life, while I am in a process of either pity, denial, or a combination of something I haven't even figured out yet. The results are in: I have mediocrity, and there is no cure.

"You're mediocre and ordinary? Of course, there's a cure!" You bright-eyed optimists would ring in my ear. But I'll let you know I'm an avid researcher of Web MD and have a graduate degree in Google, so I can confidently attest that mediocrity is terminal. It may not be the thing that kills you, but you'll die with it.

"No one's life turns out the way they envision it. You're never going to be what you thought you'd be when you were ten. Life doesn't work like that for people, except for James Ryan," my mom tried in vain to talk me down from another existential crisis.

She was right. James Ryan was more mature and worldly at ten years old than I will ever be as a middle-aged adult. Every day he would waltz into our fourth-grade classroom dressed like he was ready for court, while the rest of us barely looked bathed. We were allowed to sit in bean bag chairs while the teacher read to us. This was where most of us took our "I'm not a baby!" afternoon naps, but not James. He sat upright in his chair because it offered better lumbar support, and he was concerned about poor posture. He mocked standardized testing. His favorite TV show was Seinfeld. If anyone knew what they were going to do and how their life would look, it was him. Any parent could have looked at that kid and said, "without a doubt, James Ryan will live in Washington DC and become a fair and equitable judge".

Do you know what he's doing now? He's an attorney. I wouldn't be surprised if he's on the 2032 U.S. presidential ballot, perfect posture in all.

People have passions, but I've never really had one, with the exception of writing. I get burnt out too easily to be completely passionate and invested in something. I don't have any real hobbies either. Not because I'm lazy, but for the same reason – do I really like something enough to invest a whole lot of time and money into it? Especially when I could be getting sucked down a rabbit hole of conspiracy theories on Wikipedia or looking up dogs to potentially adopt? Nothing has struck me enough to do so.

Have I spent hours searching Zillow listings in cities I've never heard of in Florida? Sure. Am I okay with spending three hours in an Ikea, quietly criticizing my own home design choices in the face of such spectacular Swedish decor? Yes, of course. Can I be disciplined enough to learn a sport, an instrument, or how to run without sounding like a dying goose in midsummer? That's where I draw the line.

Thinking about my journey and myself, I realized that I have lived my life as if it were a buffet. Since I was a child, I'd take a little of this and a little of that not much unlike a trip to Golden Corral. I played basketball just long enough to realize I wasn't going to be Michael Jordan, and if I'm not naturally inclined, I want no part of it. I played a few instruments, but my middle school's music department would use the term "played" very, very loosely. It was more of me simulating playing the flute out of fear of failing the class.

I was in martial arts. I got a purple belt (that's good, right?), and called it a day. I dabbled in birdhouse making until it occurred to me that I don't really like birds and I don't want them to think it's okay to take up residence in my yard. I ran track, if by 'ran' we say I showed up for the concession stand hotdogs and hid in the porta-potties when my race was up.

The first time I remember feeling truly conflicted was at science camp hosted at the University of Michigan when I was 12. Yeah, I know...science camp. You had to apply to be accepted into one of the programs, and the exclusivity of that alone made it appeal to me. I picked the genetics program for no reason other than I thought I'd get to use a microscope or telescope, whatever kind of scope scientists in the movies got to use. What I didn't anticipate is that it's not "camp", it's just school during the summer. Who signs up for that?

The counselors - college students who I believed to be as equally lame as I was for spending their summer in school - would always ask us what we planned to do.

"What do you mean, what do I plan to do? Like today?" And the hell of it all is, every one of those girls had an answer. I figured I'm in the genetics program so I have to say something involving medicine. "I want to be a doctor".

Nope. That wasn't enough for them. They wanted more details, a resume, a cover letter of my life and intentions. "What type?"

...There's more than one type? "Pediatrician". This was laughable because I hated blood, and even more than that, I hated kids even while I was one. But they wanted an answer, and it was the only kind of doctor I could think of. What was I doing at science camp?

I spent that summer with brainiacs who sat around the lunch table wondering if hunger originated in your brain or your stomach. "Who cares?" I thought to myself. There's a Starbucks I had never been to but heard a lot of good things about right across the street! We also had this amazingly exotic restaurant experience called "Mongolian BBQ" and if there was any reason to get up and trek to science camp, it was for that. I had to pretend my future ambitions were to attend the prestigious University of Michigan and pursue medicine - pediatrics - and how truly fascinated I was with DNA and pea plants, and tell me again how you manage to have a 7.0 GPA?

This was not the place for me, but it made my parents proud thinking their wildcard offspring was working on her future Noble Prize in Medicine.

My point is that I like to dabble. I never wanted to get swept up in something, and then risk missing out on something else. Some may call that "noncommittal", but I affectionately refer to myself as having a lustful spirit. A healthy, eclectic appetite for all life has to offer – food or otherwise.

Some people are born with passion in their veins, and in turn they become titans of industry. We need people who are invested enough in their passions that they don't mind spending 10 years becoming a doctor. It used to embarrass me that I didn't have much of an idea of where I wanted to be or who I wanted to become. But whose job is it to decide what my merit is strictly based on what I do or what my hobbies are?

Andrew dies, my life goes up in flames, and now I'm forced to re-examine who I am. I thought I had an idea of what my life would be like at 36, but my husband performing an Irish exit in the middle of our adulthood really threw a wrench into things.

Self-examination often leads to a bit of a crisis for me. I get down on myself for not being dedicated, a savant of any variety, or at the very least disciplined. So, in the interest of rediscovering myself, I have made a list of my immediate hobbies. It goes a little something like this:

Reading (but not subscribing to) conspiracy theories, being widowed, greeting dogs before I greet humans, finding new places to display my husband's urn, going to the theatre specifically for the previews and concessions, being pretentious about things like science camp, and frequenting 'choose your own adventure' restaurants like Mongolian BBQ.

SIX

Love Struck

"I'm probably going to marry him," I giddily bounced into my sister's room to deliver the joyous news.

I was 23, fresh home from the expensive experiment of my life that was living in Chicago. "He laughs at my jokes," I gushed.

"Then yes, absolutely marry him," Kris could be counted on to be enthusiastic when the time called for it, but above all else, she was levelheaded and did her best to ground me.

Chris was sort of thrust into my life when I moved home. I had been hanging about with old grade school friends, and he was part of the package. The entire group of friends would go and do the same things every night, and it became almost impossible to not be attracted to him. Not in a love at first sight kind of way, perhaps because I had known him for so long. It was a feeling that took time to develop.

Night after night until finally, in a drunken stupor, I confided to my new bathroom best friend – "I think I like him?"

"Like him? Or like, like him?" she shouted, hugging me in the way only drunk girls who meet in a bathroom do.

Here's the thing about me: I have these moments of complete nervous anxiousness. They're infinitesimal existential seizures of thought. *Am I really here? Am I really alive?* There are moments when I will be in the middle of a fun time that requires no thought process at all, and I'll be stunned into oblivion of consciousness. And when I'm not thinking such things, I'm contemplating useless information – "do I really support the use of the oxford comma? Examine this query further". Like ticker taper constantly scrolling through my mind is a voice that is quietly interrupting my life at all times, reminding me to earn my right to be a human.

That's what happened on the way to dinner for the first time alone with Chris. It took several drinks before I could coherently form sentences that were ripe to my personality, and forget the nagging thoughts of my existence and the "what did it all mean?!" of the universe. When you have this affliction, you learn to cope. You have to, or you become a social pariah.

What I found, which was probably why I was genuinely attracted to him, is that when I was with Chris, my mind learned to ease out a bit. And our personalities, both brash and sarcastic, blended well. For the first time as a quasi-adult human, someone else made me feel secure in myself. That was both a foreign feeling and a relief.

I'd go back and tell you the middle parts – the scenes that would make up most of a romantic comedy, where we figure each other out and how it took several months before we ever kissed – but that's not the point of all of this. I won't leave you hanging. This was not a love story.

The end came hard and swift. A punch in the gut as we remained friends, but he moved on to other girls and I'd have to play my Oscar worthy performance of the girl who did not care.

"Unrequited love is a bitch," I slouched onto my sister's bed defeated, months after the liaison began.

"So, the wedding is off?" She closed her Mac book and gave my heartache her full attention.

A few Sundays later, I took my bruised heart and ego to the bowling alley for our beer league. Kris, along with our friends Phyllis and Jessica, made up the mildly competitive bowling team called the Funky Cold Medinas. We were always guaranteed last place, but also guaranteed to have the flyest shirts. It was a lovely distraction from my self-loathing to be surrounded by clouds of smoke, and the geriatric super team – 9 Pin Classics. They were the average age of 80 and used to whoop our asses every week. The girls and the Classics listened as I went over every agonizing detail. I thought I pushed so hard for things to happen that I didn't take time to consider maybe they weren't for me. Time and circumstances proved that I was a hard person to love.

"Or maybe you just don't allow people to love you? You do that a lot," Phyllis said nonchalantly, everyone nodding in agreement.

"The universe sends us what we need at the right time, and it's our job to wade through the crap to know what is right," Kris said in between bites of burnt waffle fries.

"Mmm," I chewed over the thought, chin in my hand.

"What?"

"Nothing."

"What? Say it."

"It's nothing. What are we talking about?" The words just tumbled out. I was a lamb in a time of lions - completely vulnerable and lost.

"We're talking about life," Kris shrugged and then got up to bowl.

I moped, looking down the bowling alley and laid eyes on the most attractive bowler in a Hollister polo I had ever seen. His crisp, white Air Force Ones blinded me from down the lanes. He muttered something to himself as he walked back from the spare he bowled and glanced down the alley. Our eyes met fortuitously, and my heart leapt into my throat a bit. It wasn't love at first sight. It wasn't a burning infatuation. It was my soul saying, 'a-ha there you are'. In my head I made a mental note to go home and watch the bowling scene from Grease 2 over again because this all felt very cinematic.

I stole the stained score sheet out from under the pitcher of beer and mini tacos to figure out who the mystery bowler was. Lane 16. Andrew Oubeck. "Nice to meet you, Andrew." I thought to myself, "My heart is yours forever."

SEVEN

Cope

I'm up late reorganizing closets for the second time this month. This is largely due to me perpetually living at the corner of anxiety and OCD. I'd like to ~~blame~~ thank my mom for this habit of needing things clean and in order. One of the memories seared into my brain from growing up was the terror we affectionately refer to as 'Saturday morning cleanings'. My sister Kris and I would awake to the anxiety-inducing sounds of Vern Gosdin or Tom Petty & the Heartbreakers and exchange a knowing look. We were going to be cleaning the entire house and our eardrums were going to bleed while we did it.

There was nothing to make me want to feign an illness more than hearing the opening chords of The Chain by Fleetwood Mac at 7 am mixed with the pungent smell of bathroom cleaner. We knew it was going to be a day from hell. Even Kris, who had no consciousness before the age of nine, reports her PTSD is highly triggered at the mere mention of Fleetwood's Rumours album. I suppose it's more nature than nurture in our case. I used up all the 'neat and tidy' genes, while there were slim pickings for my sister. She has tall, long legs, and a MENSA qualifying brain. While she beats me in the ways that matter to most people, I am the sister you can visit unannounced and eat off my freshly mopped floor. So really - who is the real winner here?

My life is out of control if anything is out of place or messy. This, coupled with the dance I've been doing with agoraphobia and wild insomnia since Andrew died, makes for no shortage of things to do: clean, reorganize, fix, demolish and resurface, and paint the vinyl siding in the middle of the night.

KG chastised me from the clutter of her bedroom floor, "Mom you need to have fun and stop cleaning".

"Well for starters darling child, I wouldn't have to clean all day if you'd exist in a perpetual state of cleanliness and we didn't have thousands of dogs in this house," I gestured wildly. After shaking my head and reorganizing the toilet paper stock I had been proudly building up, I realized I do need to cool it.

Realizing I need to cool it should have been my first resolution back in '98, when my favorite hobby at the time was organizing and sweeping out my locker. I'd stare at the classroom clock, waiting for the bell to ring so that I could race to the locker to ensure it was pristine. If you're wondering if I was super cool in middle school, I'll let my locker tidiness speak for itself.

My main, completely rational fear is that there is some show that will be premiering on HGTV, and I was somehow secretly picked to be on it. After all, my basic Target decor and recently steam mopped floors beneath the walls that Hobby Lobby built are 'Must See TV' if I've ever seen it.

The issue with this notion is that if perchance HGTV wanted to bust through my door to film the luxury that is my entire Pier 1 clearance section inspired homestead, I would not answer the door. They'd have to call in advance. And the trouble with that is, I don't answer my phone. I'm a typical millennial. If you call me on the phone, I will throw it out the window. Phones are meant for texting and email - purely written words so I can judge your spelling and have a paper trail if we ever mutually wind up in court. One time I answered when my sister called, and she legitimately thought something was wrong. *"Are you ok? Why are you answering?"* The last time I answered my phone, my husband died. So, excuse me if I like to keep it strictly T-9 texting over here.

If HGTV is not coming over, and I'm not expecting company or opening my door even if someone decides to pop in, why do I have to have everything to my standard of perfection? Am I going to care

20 years from now if my hall closet was Instagram worthy organized? But then my brain shouts at me: 'YOU MAY RUN FOR MAYOR ONE DAY! YOU MAY HAVE TO RELEASE RECORDS OF YOUR LIVING ROOM CONFIGURATION!'. Illogical, but also...*is it?*

This hyper-fixation on organization was exacerbated by Andrew dying. My own mortality is now always operating in one of the hundreds of tabs left open in my brain. It bears repeating that while it may not be HGTV busting down my door, it would be my poor family who has to rummage through all my crap if I die before I have time to organize it all. And if whatever it was that took me out didn't fully kill me, the embarrassment of my house being messy would finish the job.

Every few weeks I perform a systematic walk through of my house to assess what kind of pigsty I would be leaving behind if I were to die. I update my passwords and remind my mom where to find them in case 'this is it'. I realize this is probably traumatic for them – wondering if I am doing this because I am in a dark place again or if it's just the goofy weirdo with a touch of OCD rearing her lovable head?

In any case, social media does nothing to help matters. When I'm not busy cleaning, I'm aimlessly scrolling through my phone looking at other people's perfectly curated homes and photos of families in matching hues of beige on beaches. Holding hands and fake laughing, and they probably don't have a dog who wants to mark every square inch of their house. They probably have found a system that works for them to organize their shoes. How did they get it all figured out?

"You're cleaning to avoid your feelings," my therapist Mary said to me, from across the screen. I was happy to move our sessions to zoom because the office made me uncomfortable. I spent most of the time admiring the incredible molding and built in shelves and trying to memorize which books were displayed. The other half of the time I was focused on where my body was positioned and how to take up the least amount of space, while still sitting comfortably.

"I have to clean. I'm so anxious and the messiness makes it worse," I tell her, relieved she couldn't see beyond my screen to the things out of place in my dining room.

"You are not your feelings. You need to learn to sit with them. You are not anxious – things make you feel anxious," I nodded my head. What she, and the mental health side of TikTok preached to me was right. I never considered how deeply entrenched I was in my feelings. "We need to work on separating self from emotions".

"That seems quite difficult," I admitted.

"Very much so. It takes uncomfortable practice, and it's something you'll have to do for the rest of your life," I rolled my eyes. It was like being told I needed to fix my diet. Another lifestyle change when it just seemed easier to spend 4 hours cleaning my kitchen to avoid my grief and eat Burger King chicken fries for dinner.

"I'll give it the old college try," I promised.

I like to blame the outlandish obsession with organization and cleaning on coping with grief, but it's always been ingrained in me. I may not be athletic, punctual, disciplined, or good natured – but you can take it to the bank that if I die today, you can have my wake here tomorrow morning without so much as needing to run a broom over the floor. A pristine legacy to leave, indeed.

EIGHT

Chicago

Before I moved to Chicago, I knew beyond the shadow of a doubt that I was a big city girl. Nothing would be more quintessentially me than running down a busy city block to get a coffee before catching a subway train to somewhere important. I thought there was nothing for me in the streets of Southeastern Michigan suburbia where I grew up. There are only so many times you can go to the movie theatre and eat at White Castle before you begin to yearn for something more. It took approximately four hours of living in Chicago for me to learn I was wrong.

I was nineteen and irresponsible, and I didn't realize parking was a monumental issue that required permits, money, and forethought. In fact, the first weekend I lived there, my roommate Gina and I parked her car in a Best Buy parking garage.

"We'll just leave it here over the weekend, surely they won't notice if it's here a few days," We laughed ignorantly, basking in the joy of thinking we had cheated the system. An impound payment and several hundred dollars in parking tickets later, I began to wonder why anyone would want to leave the suburbs where they had perfectly good driveways to pull into every night.

I can just picture the scene to anyone observing: our broke asses merrily flitting along the city streets in Old Navy two dollar flip flops, asking for lease information of multimillion dollar high rises because delusion is not a city in Europe. Maybe I was a big city girl, but it was in another timeline. One where I was incredibly wealthy and didn't have to worry about peasant tasks like laundry, parking, and grocery shopping.

That's not to say Chicago isn't dear to my heart. When you cross the Skyway toll bridge and get your first glimpse of the skyline, no matter how many times you see it, excitement fills your bones. The air of possibility and energy reverberates out of the city like a bomb and a shock wave hits you. It's why so many songs are written as ode to Chicago.

I must have not shut up about how special the city was because when it came time to make our relationship legal and bring the government into our union as a 'throuple', Andrew packed up my mom and

Kris, and we headed to the city on the lake for a weekend of hot dogs, deep dish pizza and a marriage proposal.

Did you know the first Ferris wheel in the world debuted in Chicago at the World's Columbian Exposition of 1893? The Ferris wheel at Navy Pier was added in 1995 modeled as inspiration of that first wheel. We made our way over to ride it, and I took notice that Andrew was more nervous than his baseline quietness. "If you're afraid of heights we really don't need to do this," I said, thinking of the hot dogs awaiting us if we skipped the ride.

"You know you're special to me, right?"

Those words, the way he said them. They're forever etched in my brain. Is he breaking up with me on a Ferris wheel, I wondered? It'd be a new approach to ending a relationship but can't say I don't respect it.

"Will you marry me?" He pulled out the perfect ring, one I would have picked out for myself. He knew my style; he knew what was important to me. I couldn't hug him hard enough, and we excitedly couldn't wait for the damn wheel to get to the bottom so I could tell my mom and sister. I hung over the side of the cart shouting at them, "we're getting married!". I must have looked like a hungry rottweiler at high noon, hanging out of a car window.

I can't go to Chicago now and see the Ferris wheel without crying. I still see him there – 28 years old, blue plaid shirt and aviator sunglasses on. Smiling, happy and hopeful with the rest of his life ahead of him. There's me, gazing in amazement at the most perfect engagement ring Kay Jewelers ever crafted. Something I never thought would happen to me – an anxious mess of a human who was hard to love. He filled all the holes that were burned deep into my soul, and in that moment, everything was perfect.

NINE

Dark Blue

He was shades of blue.

His navy-blue hat he never went without. For someone so finnicky about how his hair was cut, the hat was a permanent fixature. His light blue button up shirts he wore every chance he could - the ones he had to be bullied into trying on in the first place. In 2010 he and I were in Urban Outfitters with my sister Kris, who was wildly ahead of us in fashion.

"Try this plaid shirt," she held it up to him. He stalked out of the store after she made the request too many times, pouting on the bench. He was strictly dedicated to his Hollister polo shirts and baggy jeans, and he'd be damned before he'd sport some hipster threads. A few months later, blue plaid was all he would wear.

He was dark blue. His long-sleeved work uniform he wore every day - the one labeled 'Andrew', in cursive over his right side. Smudged in grease and the smell of steel in the fabric from the hours he spent at the plant. The blue shirt they cut from him to try to save his life. The once blue work clothes, now soaked in red, tossed away.

He was the accent wall of turquoise blue we painted the living room of our first home. The blue of painters tape he didn't need to use because he was so precise, so careful. He didn't splatter or make mistakes, he was exact.

"Please do not paint while I'm at work, just let me do it," he made me promise. Everything was better because of him. He kept me from putting forty different nails in the wall to hang one picture frame because he'd take the time to measure. One New Year's weekend, KG and I spent the entire time eating snacks in the bedroom watching enough Paw Patrol to make a dog salivate, while Andrew redid the kitchen. We emerged to find it looking like an upscale Red Lobster, exactly what I had asked for but was too lazy to do the work.

He was the blue UNO card, the game he loved to play with his daughter. He was Chuck Taylor Converse shoes, his favorite pair faded blue with wear. He was the blue of the riding lawn mower, lifting KG up to help drive and making laps in the backyard. Letting her steer, not knowing he was creating memories we'd cling to like a life raft in the storm his absence left behind.

Blue like the water we live by. The freighters would come through and I'd hear them from the back window, and you could smell the water even though you can't see it from here. Kind of like him.

I have to close my eyes to see his blue now. I'm surrounded by only red.

Red for the cardinals that hang out in my tree and stare at me in an uncanny way when I walk outside. The statues and pictures of them that people kept buying me, telling me he was still near us. Red for the anger I still carry around with nowhere to go. Red for the blood I cannot get out of my head.

TEN

Therapy Dog

Recently, I visited a psychic medium. She stared at my tattooed arm and deduced I was probably suffering some sort of malady of loss. "He's here with you. He's telling me he is always with you at your house".

My blood ran cold. "He knows," I whispered. He knows I brought home another dog.

A few months after Andrew died, I lost my 14-year-old rottweiler who I raised from a puppy. She was brittle and her hips were bad, and it was just another blow to my already barely beating heart. If there's one thing about me though, it's that I'm going to bring home another dog.

My first Newfoundland experience was with my friend Chris' big old boy Brutus. I couldn't believe how larger than life this dog was, and in the back of my mind I always thought I needed one. Just to hug and let him sit on my lap and say, 'who is a big baby?" every night. Andrew quickly put the kibosh on another dog, especially a gigantic one.

I already had to make a supreme court level case in defense of us keeping our first dog, Charles Barkley. Charles was a free farm puppy we adopted a few months after living together, and it felt like we were playing house.

"Aww he's our baby," I'd say, as he shit all over our apartment and Andrew cleaned it up. Despite training, neutering, and antipsychotic medication, Charles never mellowed out. He will bark himself hoarse. He hates the sight of delivery trucks. He's been uninvited to multiple dog parks.

"No more dogs," Andrew repeated to me daily.

If Andrew is indeed hanging around like Casper the friendly ghost, then he knows I've brought home more animals. And that means he has watched as Muggsy, the big newfoundland, has destroyed our floors and eaten a couch. And that means, he is high key pissed.

Muggsy was named after Charlotte Hornets legend Muggsy Bogues and joined her brother Charles Barkley to add to my dog roster of NBA greats. What Muggsy (the dog, not the person) lacks in basic restraint, she makes up for in gentle sweetness. We got her to be a therapy dog for KG a few months after Andrew died.

"This is just what we need," I manically announced as I drove through the back hills of Amish country, almost flipping my car over in an attempt to navigate without a GPS. The drive to get Muggsy was a metaphor for the adventure we were about to embark on in training her.

"She'll be a lot of work," my mom, sensible as always, warned. I shook my head dismissively. She still had the video on her phone from a few weeks previous when I declared "do not ever let me get another dog" as I scraped dog shit off my new shoes.

Grown newfoundland dogs are exactly what you read about – big, gentle giants who are the most lovable creatures on the planet. Those are grown-ups though. Puppy through two-year-old newfs are an entirely different beast. They will beat your ass up Ivan Drago style. They will eat everything, up to and including Apple pens you take your eyes off of for two seconds. They'll break off their leash, freshly groomed, and run away to a muddy ditch and take their own bath because fuck you that's why! They'll have bloody diarrhea, chronic ear infections, severe allergies and ten thousand dollars later they'll crawl into your poor folk lap and give you a hug. So yeah, she was worth it.

Every day I must walk the pair of dogs down our cul-de-sac and pass the house with three miniature poodles who Charles has beef with. We call them "Janet & the boys". The house has an electric fence, but Janet – the leader of the tripod of poodles – gives zero fucks and will be electrocuted to death just to scrap with Charles. There is no way around this house or these bullies. My choice is to either not walk the dogs and let them burn the house to the ground with energy or walk them and risk a dog fight club.

Janet & the boys have a human – we'll call her Ethel – she is around seventy and is lovely. She always wants to chat when we're walking by, and seemingly doesn't understand the Michael Vick situation that is playing out before us. Being impolite is my kryptonite. I just can't do it. I have no choice but to stop and respond when she speaks to me. With an eagle eye, I spot her on the corner under her gardening hat, pulling weeds like the angel she is, surrounded by the hounds of hell. Like clockwork, the following will happen:

- Janet & the boys smell fresh meat and start doing what can only be described as pushups to warm up for the rumble in the jungle

- Ethel approaches the street, waving at me from a distance. I motion to the dogs as if to say to Ethel, "if I come any closer, the blood will be on your hands."

- She'll yell over to me, "What is your dog's name again?"

I scream her name. "Muggsy"

"Murphy??"

"No, MUGGSY"

"MUFFY??"

"Yes, Muffy," Dogs are baring teeth. Shrill barks are lighting up the neighborhood.

"Aww hi, Midgey! She's beautiful," it's then she takes notice of the scene before us. She shrugs underneath her gardening hat. "They're just talking to each other."

I smile and wave as I'm dragging the dogs away, mapping out a new route in my head, cutting through yards to avoid the poodle's wrath. I considered calling an Uber to get home to safety.

Muggsy is the stronger one who I can barely control, but Charles is the one with a chip on his shoulder and anger issues. It's as if he's always trying to prove himself, especially to dogs who are smaller than him. The way Hannibal Lector had to be restrained in a dolly with a mask over his face is the same way I'm forced to take Charles literally anywhere. He was banned for life from multiple groomers, an unfortunate one where, in a fit of rage, he ripped the cages off the wall.

It sounds like I'm a bad pet owner, and I'm not. But I can tell you that pets reflect your own psyche. Muggsy is the sensitive, namaste side of me. Charles is the mentally ill part. And when you add three stuck up poodles to that mix, it's a deadly combination.

If Andrew is around, he's surely watching from the porch as I drag the two furry idiots home, away from the chaos that only miniature poodles can cause. He's shaking his head and muttering to himself, "that's what you get. I said no more dogs".

ELEVEN

Sisterhood

Somehow in the chaos of Andrew dying, my sister teleported from where she lived an hour north of Detroit and made it to the hospital where he died in less than twenty minutes. I suppose crises and emergencies can do that, but it always alarms me when I think back to how fast she had to be driving to get there at that time. She was there as I walked out of the hospital and into the rainy Thursday evening, unsure of what to do or where to go.

I lost my husband, but she lost her brother-in-law. They were close in so many ways I never was to Andrew. They were both patient, grounded, and well-balanced.

Kris would walk in the door and say, "Hello Mountain Drew," handing him a Mountain Dew.

He'd say, "They call me 'Drew Do' cause 'Drew Do everything'.".

"Nobody calls you that," Kris would tease him.

"If you die, I'd just marry your sister," Andrew would jokingly reassure me whenever I'd go over my contingency plan for my impending death for the thousandth time. "It's the easiest scenario for everyone".

She lived with us for a short time after finishing graduate school. She was like our second child. We'd load up the car with KG, Kris, and the diaper bag and we'd 'hit the strip' - which was our affectionate way of referring to the local Target and Michaels stores. When Andrew chose to cash out on life as the world was shutting down, Kris didn't think twice about moving in with me for a few months. She packed up some of her best Instagram photographable dishes, her cat, and a yoga mat, and moved into the once designated nursery for the subsequent babies we'd never have.

We put together enough puzzles and built enough Legos to give us arthritis. She made me into a vegetarian with her "999 things you can do with some chickpeas" dinners. She played with KG, read to her, and generally made sure I stayed alive long enough for me to get my shit together. I shudder to think what would have become of us if we didn't have Kris in our lives because there was a time when we almost broke up as sisters.

It was 2009. Graphic t-shirts of Nirvana, low rise jeans, and velour jumpsuits were the official uniform of the day. One afternoon we found ourselves in a most charitable mood and decided to take the dinner burden off our overworked mother and handle it ourselves. We were bopping along to a Flo Rida banger, headed to the grocery store to gather the delicacies needed to carry out our gourmet dining experience. Cooking for Kris and I in those days meant *'don't worry about dinner tonight mom, we're making cold subs'.* This also meant accidentally buying cabbage instead of lettuce because neither one of us could tell the difference.

Sometime during this trip, I bought a large, snack sized bag of Hershey's Cookie and Cream bars. It was explicitly understood that this contraband was mine and mine alone. It had nothing to do with the wholesome, Iron Chef level family meal prep we were about to undertake. *"If you want something for you, get it yourself. This booty is all mine,"* my future root canals in the making yelled at her.

Outside of the store, it is a monsoon. Kris, like a stealth gazelle, grabs a few bags and jumps into the car leaving me to throw the rest in the trunk and return the cart. I digress, but if you do not return your cart at a grocery store, please take this as a personal invitation from me to escort your eyes off this book. Barring any medical reason, if you're not walking the 50 feet over to the cart corral, you are leading to the decline of modern society. Do better.

I jumped in the car to a Gene Wilder horror. Do you remember the scene in Willy Wonka & The Chocolate Factory where Augustus

Gloop is gluttonously killin' the chocolate river? That paints an adequate portrait for what Kris was doing to MY Hershey's chocolate. She sat there like a greedy little German boy, slurping up my bounty.

"You could have picked out your own!" I screamed, as only a 23-year-old young lady does when she sees her sister eating her candy.

"It was a few pieces, sorry," Kris shrugged and rolled the bag up.

I'll admit, I'm a lot calmer in my old age. It has brought wisdom, and of course, cavities due to the candy addiction I suffered. But in those days, my rage burned red like a solar flare. I drove down the road a bit and then pulled over.

"Finish it." I demanded as I parked the car, shoving the 20 ounce bag of chocolate in her face.

"What? Go home." She refused.

"Nope. You're going to eat every bite of that or you can walk home. You want to be greedy, then go ahead and enjoy," The hurricane gale winds pounded the car. She had no choice. We sat on the side of the road for twenty minutes. With every bite, she cried and begged for mercy.

"You have issues, Danielle!" she yelled at me.

"Yeah well, this is hurting me more than it is hurting you," I cried as she crumpled up the now empty bag and tossed it at me. My stomach gurgled with emptiness and revenge.

"I'm telling mom when we get home," she threatened. Just what our mother needed - her adult children, bickering over candy.

We got home, threw the cabbage subs together in front of our confused parents like it was some sort of anger filled, sandwich hibachi restaurant, and didn't speak the rest of the night. We've both changed a lot since then. I'm not a vengeful maniac, and Kris is a vegan so there would be no stealing of milk chocolate for her nowadays.

I'm not sure where we'd be without my sister. She's my true north for my moral compass. She is KG's best friend. For the record, I'm so fortunate to have her. But if she ever eats my candy again, so help me God...

TWELVE

Constipation

Often, we think we are knowledgeable when it comes to a particular subject because we've dabbled in experience with it. It's not until a subject is completely exacerbated do we realize we truly understood nothing about it. That's how life goes, I suppose. We continue to learn that what we previously knew was dull and dim in comparison to our enlightened now.

That is how constipation was for me. Whenever I'd hear the word, I would think, "well you ate too much cheese. Push a little harder and stop complaining". Because isn't how someone handles a bowel movement a good indicator of that person's stance on life? What type of person needs a medical diagnosis for a time when it's hard for them to go to the bathroom? Buck up, bear down, and persevere. Be steadfast in your duty. That's the only way that shit is coming out.

Up until that point, the night of America's birthday, my opinion of constipation was guided by my naiveté and lack of personal experience. It was around 9 pm when I decided it might be time to use the facilities. After all it had been...9 days.... since I had previously gone. How does one go 9 days without pooping? It's easy when it's not something you really keep track of. It's not like I had an advent calendar in my bathroom. Things happen, you get busy, you forget you haven't moved your bowels. That doesn't make me any less of an adult, alright?

I was also suffering from another malady during that time - pregnancy. In the 35 books and informative websites I had indulged in, I must have skipped the rather large section regarding being constipated. After 25 minutes in the bathroom and making no progress, it occurred me to that this was going to go from being classified as a "bathroom problem" to a "bathroom situation". It's like moving the terror threat level from yellow to orange - it's time to lock down the borders. Even though we were married and with child, Andrew and I were not the sort of couple who would discuss bathroom mischief. I wanted to see this through alone.

The pain I experienced can only be described as fear that I was giving birth. It had to be a developed fetal head that was putting that pressure on me without moving any further down. How could poop possibly be that powerful? I panicked that I was destined to be on a show on cable television that featured women who gave birth in the toilet because they thought they just had to take a crap. And then there'd be the embarrassment I'd suffer when the day would inevitably come, and I'd have to explain to KG her birth story. Because there was no way this was just a matter of being constipated. It had to be something a little more sinister than some fecal matter.

40 minutes passed and after googling some at home remedies, 'DIY Shitting for Dummies', and having no luck, I knew I had to call my mom or a hearse. One of which had to solve my dilemma.

My mother and Kris, cloaked by the darkness of night, made their way to a pharmacy for some midnight stool softeners and suppositories. I had some working knowledge of suppositories before. Luckily, I had been friends with a girl who used them recreationally, and I understood the nature of the beast. Put it in and get ready for a rumble in the jungle because it's going to hurt. Waves of cramps washed over me. Sweating, unable to sit and forced to walk without bending my knees, I circled my house, praying to any deity that would accept me for something would happen.

When the entire box of suppositories failed to yield any results, and a phone call to my doctor didn't help, it was time to go to the hospital. My shame and humiliation took a backseat to the fear I had of having to sit down in a car to get there. When you have a softball sized brick of poop at the base of your anal passage, you begin to think of ways to die that would be far superior to your current circumstance.

You also begin to go over every single piece of food you've eaten over the past 9 days that lead to your predicament. Was that chicken salad and Swiss sandwich the catalyst? Who is really to blame here?

Walking into the emergency room was, to say the least, unequivocally embarrassing. When you think of things you never want to have to say, one of them is, "I'm 26 years old, I need to see a medical professional to scrape some shit out of my butthole". After ruling out that it wasn't a "pregnancy" emergency, they lead me and my band of equally ashamed family members to a curtained room in the ER. There, mother, sister, and husband stood around as I leaned over the hospital bed and began to shake. My fate finally occurred to me, and the terror set in - there was only one way to get the crap out, and that was for something or someone to go in. God bless the faithful departed.

When the doctor and resident walked in, I explained my situation - pregnant, yadda yadda, not responsible enough to realize I hadn't gone to the bathroom in a protracted amount of time, save me from myself. I know not what I do.

I was then forced to climb onto the gurney and expose the base of the issue.

"Well do you want to go in there and see what the blockage is?" The doctor instructed the intern. What a way to spend a national holiday

- checking an adult's rectum to make sure there wasn't any foul play afoot.

"Oh yeah, that's definitely impacted feces," the resident withdrew his hand, snapping his glove in disgust and defeat.

"Enema!" Said the doctor.

My body began to violently shake with trepidation. Enemas can be comical and fun to joke about, until you are at the receiving end of one. But what was worse? My bowels being ripped apart from the pain and pressure of constipation, or a hose featuring molasses and saline being forcefully shoved in? There was no easy answer. Before I could work out in my head what was about to happen, a nurse and an aide came in with a brown IV bag and long hose.

And then, it began. It was in, things were happening, I was simultaneously crying and taking the lord's name in vain. My embarrassed and disgusted family waited on the other side of the curtain, undoubtedly both hearing and smelling the terror that was happening to me.

If Doc Brown showed up at my door today with a DeLorean, I would say gun it to 88 mph, and take me back to July 3. I would voluntarily suck down 6 gallons of prune juice and MiraLAX.

"Ok now the longer you hold it in, the more it will clear you out," the nurse shouted at me, quickly escaping the room.

They say you see a white light just before you die. Your mind becomes very clear, and your life plays out before your eyes. Left alone on the bed, letting the waves of pain crash over my body, this happened to me. Trips to Disneyworld, dance recitals, Franco American macaroni and cheese dinners...my life was like a peaceful movie, leaving everything around me feeling Zen. Roughly 60 seconds had passed, and the movie ended. The post-credit scene was one of me hovering over myself in a hospital bed. Angels are shaking their heads. *"How'd she wind up like this? How is that much poop even possible?"* I realized I had to make it to the portable potty they brought in, or the poor nurse's aide would have a shit storm to clean up.

Andrew, who had made a legal pledge to be by side and had at least a little bit of responsibility in putting me in that physical predicament, stood far away from the madness that was ensuing. "I'm sorry, you know I'll throw up," he apologized.

My sister, the one with whom I shared a womb, wanted no part of the Tarantinoesque horror playing out before her. I weakly limped alone to the potty, cradling my arm around my belly. Fetal KG was relaxed as the evening's activities lulled her to sleep. Like a ray of sunshine, my mother emerged from the curtain. "I will help you," she gagged.

It was then I learned the meaning of true unconditional love. The measure of a mother's heart is never fully tested until you are given an enema and seated upon a portable potty on the 4th of July.

Just as quickly as the nightmare began, it was over. The relief made me cry out in joy. "Glory to god!" I wanted to broadcast it over the hospital speakers. It wasn't without sacrifice though. After cleaning myself off and surveying the damage that had been done to the potty, the bed, and surrounding medical staff, I arose from the room like a phoenix from the ashes. I had survived constipation. I had another badge of merit to add to my girl scout sash of life.

3 and a half hours from the initial discovery of my medical dilemma, we were on our way home with a discharge instruction sheet that clearly spelled out how to take care of yourself. Stray fireworks randomly exploded in the sky as I wondered what my life would have been like if I had never experienced that. Would I continue living, believing that constipation was just a joke? An old wives' tale or myth that was passed on from Viking lords to warn against eating too much cheese.

I am not ashamed. I am an enema veteran - the few and the proud. My constipation nightmare ended that night in the emergency room. But a new kind of terror awaited me. The sort of thing that makes you question your own mortality.

Hemorrhoids - the next frontier.

THIRTEEN

Miscarried

"Here we go again," I braced myself, positive pregnancy test in my hand.

I wasn't good at being pregnant. I carried KG to term, throwing up every single day, but after that it was as if my uterus decided to go on strike.

"Nothing you can do. It's no fault of yours. Just unlucky, I guess," I'd hear. But this time felt different.

I did as I was supposed to. I bought prenatal vitamins. I choked them down even though a mere sip of water would send me on a vomiting rollercoaster. I researched unmedicated births. "I'm going hard this time," I told Andrew.

We cleared out the guest room to make way for a crib. There was a Pinterest board with French toile wallpaper and baby animal art. I signed up for baby updates. The size of a lentil, then a blueberry, a cherry. Fruit sized children. "You're holding 2 babies right now," Ken would say as she sat on my hip.

I allowed myself to feel hopeful. There was a sense of relief that maybe the second baby would be less stressful because we'd know what to expect. When I had KG, she was only the third baby I had ever held and the second diaper I had ever changed.

"What in the ever-loving hell did I get myself into?" I asked myself, as I dislocated my shoulder swinging her in her car seat because the mechanical swing didn't quite suit her highbrow taste. She liked to gaze up at the sweat and distress in my face as I swung her to slumber.

Somehow knowing I wouldn't be sleeping through the night for the next three years brought comfort because there'd be a sense of completeness to our family. The empty fourth chair at the table would be filled with something other than our discarded jackets. Someone to have a shared history with KG. She deserved a sibling – a partner in life to grow with, to argue with, to make fun of Andrew and I together when they were teenagers.

We laid there staring at the ultrasound screen, everyone silent as the technician searched for a heartbeat.

"How about we try a transvaginal ultrasound? Sometimes those babies like to give us trouble," the technician smiled slightly. "I'll grab the doctor while you get situated."

I nodded. She shut the door, and I started to cry. "She couldn't find the heartbeat. There's no heartbeat."

"You don't know that," Andrew said standing up next to me, as if closing proximity to each other would fix things.

"No, that's what it meant. There's no heartbeat," I was crying when the doctor and technician softly knocked and came back into the room.

I had been seeing this doctor for a few years and had known her briefly through working at the hospital, and she always had a calm demeanor. I had never been more grateful to have a caring doctor than at that moment.

"Danielle, I am so sorry. There is no heartbeat," they gave us some information on what would happen and then gave us some time. Andrew silently stood, handing me tissues, shocked that I was right. Part of the knowing was from being a nurse and the intuitive nature of healthcare worker's needing to read other's energy, but mostly it is the magic of motherhood. Sometimes you just know.

I thought telling KG would be one of the hardest things I'd have to tell her, but of course life has its way of making you eat your words. There'd be worse things to come. She was five years old, trying to digest the news.

"But I already told my class I'm going to be a big sister." My heart shattered with every word. She'd grow up to be many amazing things, but never a sister. I cannot give her that.

I spent the rest of the year entangled with guilt for what I was depriving her of - a built-in playmate, friend, someone to learn how to live and love with. I look at my sister and think of how lucky I am to have her, and then get a pit in my stomach when I think of KG not having that because of me. *"We're going to have to make up for what she doesn't have,"* I told Andrew, ad nauseam.

You won't be a sister, I'd think, *but you'll be the most loved daughter in the entire world. You'll have adventures, you'll never be bored. I'll never let you feel pain. We'll give you everything we have, your daddy and me.*

And now...

Here we are. Just the two of us.

She sleeps silently beside me. A sibling-less child with a dead father. With a mother who is struggling to keep it together.

"You're still the most loved daughter in the entire world," I whisper to her. *We'll have adventures together, you and me. You will have moments of boredom, frustration, pain, sadness because this is life and regardless of how much I want to, I cannot shield you from that. Sadness means you have the ability to be happy. I'm sure you'll have moments when you aren't pleased with me. I'm sure you'll wonder why life dealt you these cards.*

But beyond anything else, KG, I will give you everything I have of me for the rest of my life. You will never have to wonder if you're safe, if you're unconditionally accepted, if you're loved. I will tell you every day what you meant to your dad. You will never have to wonder how important you are.

You have all of me, and I know beyond the clouds, high in the sky, in the deep part of your heart that speaks to you - all of your daddy too.

FOURTEEN

Widow Braces

My widow's resolution was to get adult braces.

In middle school, I was the proud operator of camera three for our school news show. We would meet once a month and film at our local cable TV station. It felt like the big leagues for someone who had spent 300 hours filming themselves in the bathroom mirror with a handheld Samsung doing their best Saturday Night Live Weekend Update impressions.

Imagine my delight when my well-enunciated friend and anchor Rachel wasn't there to film one evening.

"I guess we could have Danielle do it," my teacher reluctantly suggested. I wasn't next in line because of my unpolished talent, but more so because we didn't really use camera three.

This is what the history books will write about, I thought to myself as I took my place behind the stained desk. When I am the next regional news anchor, they will say it began at this moment. I blankly read off the prompter, wishing I had at least run a brush through my hair that day before my big debut.

"Nice effort, Danielle," our teacher said to me as I bounded off the set after we finished.

"Thanks! This is what I've always wanted to do. I want to be a news anchor," I smiled. She scrunched up her nose.

"You'll have to get those teeth fixed though. News anchors have fantastic dental work," then she turned on her heels and walked away. This is when my villain era began.

My parents didn't believe in orthodontics. "They'll straighten themselves out," they'd say as if my teeth just needed time to find themselves.

I'd walk the halls of my middle school, longingly admiring my friends' braces. They'd leave school to get new brackets replaced or switch out colored rubber bands, and it all felt boastful. "They hurt," they'd complain, using wax to dull the ache.

"I'll bet, but at least you'll be employable one day," I'd reply cuttingly. It had to be hard to be friends with me in middle school. There was always some train of craziness running through my brain, and my friends were assigned a ticket they didn't ask for.

In a fit of envy one afternoon, I decided to fashion my own retainer out of paperclips. I molded them as best I could to my teeth and stuck them in my mouth just before the bell rang for dismissal. I strutted to the bus, took my place standing against the window with one leg kneeling on the seat so everyone would have a clear view of the orthodontic device I was now sporting. Did she leave school to get a new retainer? I thought they'd quietly ask amongst themselves.

We were only a few stops away from my house when the bus hit a pothole. A regular pothole would have been no trouble, but a Michigan pothole meant the bus left this plane of existence and tumbled into the seventh circle of hell and returned with no bus suspension left to speak of. A cacophony of pubescent screams filled the air as we tumbled around the bus. "That was a close one," the bus driver sneered.

It was then I realized that somehow in the ruckus, my homemade retainer had pierced through my tongue and coiled itself around it. I tried to pull it off and the pain seared through my mouth, the paperclip not budging.

"Oww!" I screamed.

"What did you do?" My friend Rachel examined the scene before her without judgment.

"It's not a retainer, it's a paperclip!" I managed to slur. I was crying now.

"Yeah. I figured that," She grimaced as she assessed my tongue. "It's turning really red. You gotta get that off."

"I can't," I cried. The bus lurched to my stop, and I ran off crying. The anticipation of looking cool was now eclipsed by a trail of blood as I scurried home in hopes my mom could remedy the emergency at hand.

After determining this possibly required hospital intervention, we drove to the nearest emergency room. I gave it a last-ditch effort to pry the tetanus-laden steel out of my tongue in the parking lot. It finally came out as I gasped with relief.

"You have to stop doing shit like this," my mom sighed, putting the car in reverse to head home.

My teeth just sort of hung out there as I developed new, more exciting things to be insecure about: my body, the sound of my voice on a voicemail, the way I organized my DVD collection. It wasn't until Andrew died did I think it was time to put this matter to bed.

"I'm 33 and I'm ready for braces, do your worst!" I proudly proclaimed to the dental assistant. I glanced around expecting to see young children crying as the brackets were tightened on their little teeth. Instead, I was met with other adults.

"I never wore my retainers," one lady said to me, pulling down her mask and revealing an uneven smile.

So, this is another lifelong thing I have to commit to, I lamented. Therapy and working on myself and exercising and wearing retainers – how do we fit all of this into our daily lives? Where is there room to just be a lazy sack of shit and binge watch Sister Wives?

18 months after my initial visit, and after several times dropping my aligner trays on sawdust floors or accidentally flushing them down a toilet, their masterpiece was complete. I looked in the mirror and my heart was full. No one is going to accuse me of having a smile that lights up a room, and I'd still never get a job as a news anchor. But it is now something I can mark off my list of "things that are wrong with me that I can fix".

FIFTEEN

Dreams

I ask my brain or the universe to dream of Andrew. It rarely happens.

I close my eyes and wake up in my own house. The midmorning sun is shining through the window. I don't remember how I got here, at the top of the stairs, but there's movement at the bottom. It's Andrew. He's walking up towards me.

"Oh my god, I thought you were dead," I say with a gasp.

"What?" He smiles slightly, one hand on the handrail.

"I had this dream that you died. It was insane," I'm hugging him, relief is washing over me. Dreams are crazy like that, how real they can feel. How thankful you are when you wake up from a terrible one.

A second later, we're downstairs in our living room. We're standing across from each other and it is nighttime. The house is dark. I can't put my finger on it, but something is off.

"Where are we?" I ask. His finger twirls around his head and upwards, as if to say, outer space. That was me. I was always up in the sky; he was always grounded Andrew.

"Where we are," I pause before answering my own question, closing my eyes to picture the scene better. "We're together. We're on a plane. To Fiji." It's cliché, but it's where we are. Over an endless ocean of cliches.

He smiles, "Go on".

"So, we're in Fiji. A nice hotel, one where they make animals out of towels to leave on your bed. Our room has doors that open to the beach. You can leave them open all night because it's Fiji and the weather is perfect and listening to the waves helps you sleep."

"It's like a sleep aid?"

"Exactly. But we wouldn't sleep," I'm smiling now, picturing the bungalow over the water. "We'd be busy walking on the beach, amazed with the stars in that hood. Because there's no light pollution. And I'd be telling you about, I don't know, NASA probably. We'd walk, hand in hand, and it'd be how it always is between us. It'd be perfect." My voice catches in my throat. "And I wouldn't be anxious on this trip, because I wouldn't have to be. Because we're finally together, on the other side of the world in paradise."

Then there's silence. The reality of where we are sets in. It's dark and cold.

"But we're here," I sigh and wipe a tear away before it has a chance to fall. "I want you to be happy. I want to be happy."

"But I'm dead," he says matter-of-factly. As the words leave his mouth, the floor starts to shutter beneath our feet and the walls slowly quake.

"I don't want you to be dead. I can stay here," I'm beginning to shout, gripping onto the photos on the walls to keep them from falling. I'm bargaining now.

"There will be a Fiji for us one day, but it's not here and it's not now," his voice is further away. There's chaos as the house - our house – starts to crumble, dissolving into itself with us inside. "You need to live."

"I can stay. I can stay," I'm screaming. I can do nothing but watch in horror as the things that made our house a home - the dishes bought at our bridal shower, the furniture we picked out together, my brooch bouquet I carried at our wedding – it's breaking apart, crashing to the floor, destroyed.

"You need to breathe!" I hear the voice of the nurse who took care of him the day he died, echoing from the hallway. She's shouting at us, at me.

"We'll be together again, but you have to go," he shoves me hard out the front door as the house collapses.

Then I wake up.

SIXTEEN

Daddy Daughter Dance

"You're going to get to go to daddy daughter dances!" I professed my unbridled excitement to Andrew as we drove home from the gender ultrasound when we found out KG was a girl. It was he, after all, who on our first date told me he couldn't wait to have a baby.

"I'm going to have a little girl; I just know it. My brother is having a boy, so I'm going to have a girl," he said over saganaki and lamb gyros.

"I don't think it works like that," I said, wondering if my irritable bowels could tolerate a round of baklava.

It was frightening to be on a date with someone who was actively admitting to wanting children. I thought we were still at the tender age where we were frightened by the prospect, but at 26, Andrew was certain of his future.

"No, I'll have a girl. I'll take her to those father daughter dances they have," he said confidently. With those words, I would have married him right then and there if he had asked. It wasn't that I wanted to be a parent – I wasn't sure if I wanted kids – but to have a partner who would willingly attend such an event? Tie me to them for eternity.

I met my own biological father in a bar on a Thursday night when I was nineteen. This is significant for several reasons. One being my bio dad was a recovering alcoholic, Jesus reborn man, and I was lost and using alcohol as a crutch to make it through young adulthood. It was terse in that I had spent the previous decade doing private eye type sleuthing to try to find him and all his secrets. This was before Al Gore invented the internet, and I had to dig in the phone book for any information. By the time he wanted to meet me, I had an established life and plans.

"It's Thursday, which is the start of our usual bar weekend. He's just going to have to meet us there and tag along," I told my mom. Also, the boy I had been desperately pining after would possibly be at the bar, so there was no way I was going to pass up the chance to awkwardly stare at him from the other side of the room as I drank bottom shelf vodka and lemonade.

It all felt like a poignant display, but one drenched in shame and embarrassment. Much like the time in the fifth grade when I, by the skin of my teeth, graduated from speech therapy. They called me up in front of thirty other ten-year-olds who salivated at the chance to make fun of me. They presented me with a certificate of completion, and it warmed my heart but also made me nervous. As a mediocre child with no discernible talent or dedication, I had to take these participation trophies where I could. The acknowledgement made me feel special, even if it was at the expense I'd pay for my peers knowing my speech was the best it was going to get and the pseudo-Boston accent I was rocking was here to stay.

I arrived that Thursday evening in my finest business casual bar attire that was popularized by the early 2000s Forever 21, and I did not reflect on the past. I was fixated on what he'd look like, what he'd think of me, and what life from this point forward would be for everyone.

He arrived with a rather large entourage and all the nervous energy one could possibly muster. "I brought reinforcements in case you were going to jump me," he shouted. I glanced around at my friends – girls in their early twenties who were there for one-dollar shots and wearing halter tops. I wasn't sure the threat level was too high.

A 6-foot tall, 45-year-old stranger with thinning hair sat before me. It wasn't what the movies portray. It was uncomfortable the same way starting a new job or going to jury duty is uncomfortable. You don't want to be here, but you hope for the best.

"What do you want to know about me?" He leaned over the table, nervously smiling.

"This tells me everything I need to know," I thought to myself. Any tact, humility and general self-awareness I may have was inherited from my mother. He took little interest in me as a person or in my life. He treated the meeting like he was a guest on Conan O'Brian, and it was his job to charm an audience. It was as if he woke up bored one day and thought, who can I talk about myself to that I haven't yet? Why don't I call that kid I've never spoken to?

I didn't care about how he'd made something of himself after a rough start or how he'd found Jesus. It wasn't very Christian in my opinion to have a child and leave the job of raising her to her mother, with little thought or apology to the consequences.

As an abandoned child, I always wondered if there was some journal he was waiting to give me of the times he wanted to talk to me but couldn't. A box of cards, perhaps, of birthdays and graduations he missed. There was nothing but narcissism, and it carved out another hole in me. I kept hope alive that there was some silent care for me, affection being kept to himself - father daughter dances he wished he could be at, but circumstances wouldn't allow for. "But I'll make it up to her!" He'd think.

But that wasn't him. And my mom was right to protect me from the cowardice that would have led to poor fatherhood attempts on his part. It wasn't until having KG did my apathy turn to rage. I looked at her, sleeping in my arms and wondered how someone could so easily abandon their duty as a parent and show no remorse?

The rage tempered with time as emotions often do. I came to terms with my issues as though they didn't matter anymore. I had married someone who was patient and kind and put his baby girl before all else. I had righted a generational wrong.

Andrew and KG never made it to a daddy daughter dance. They had their own version of 'daddy daughter date nights' when I would work late, and he'd take her to the movies or to get the biggest ice cream sundae a restaurant could serve. In a way only Andrew could, he took care of his girls from the outer stretches of beyond this life. He sent us Matthew.

SEVENTEEN

Matthews

There was a time in my life when I'd happily spend my mother's last twenty dollars on a tarot card reading. I needed someone or something to tell me what to do because I couldn't possibly trust my own judgment. Over time, however, my belief in anything that wasn't concrete waned. I couldn't put stock in magic. I had a credit score and mortgage to worry about for cripes' sake.

Imagine my surprise when I found myself sitting across from a psychic medium two years after Andrew died. She looked me over – searching for clues, I thought to myself. But as if Andrew were whispering directly in her ear Patrick Swayze in Ghost style, she began to rattle off intimate details about our life: how he died, the layout of our house, his car that sat in pieces in the garage. "It's ok to sell it," she waved me off.

"He's trying to communicate with you through the lights and the house. Are your lights flickering a lot since he transitioned?" The question made me squirm. If he was to blame for the electrical issues going on in the house, then it was safe to assume he was also responsible for the plumbing as well. A month before this, my kitchen flooded. Then, the hot water heater began leaking. A few days later, the lights went out in the kitchen. The bulbs were changed, the wiring assessed. Everything was in tip-top shape. The next day it was the lights in a different room. The TV would turn on at all hours of the day. The Ring doorbell would alert me, 'A person is at the front door', but there would be no one there. And so on and so on, until I finally screamed "what the absolute fuck???" Then it stopped.

"Who is Matthew?" A lump rose in my throat and choked the air out of me. If Andrew knows about Muggsy the dog, then he knows about Matthew.

"He was there when Andrew died," I started to cry and sweat. This was true, but what was also true was that Matthew was my now boyfriend. Partner, as I usually say because boyfriend makes me feel like I'm 14 again and chatting on AOL instant messenger.

I felt like there was an invisible string of trauma that tied him and I together. Matthew had suffered great loss in his life, and I felt seen. We went for a walk one day to talk about religion and what happens after we die, and somehow, we began talking about how half of his finger was cut off.

"I didn't even feel it. The doctor came in and the bone just looked like horsehair," he held his hand up. I couldn't stop laughing at the way he told the story. It was a deep laugh, tears piercing the sides of my eyes. I instantly felt guilty for laughing at all.

"It's okay to laugh. You're going to laugh again," he said without judgement. They refer to your person as a 'significant other', and when they're gone, that significance cannot be overstated. They're in everything you are and do. Laughing when they're dead, even months later, feels criminal.

I like to think Matthew was given to me by the universe of divine intervention. I didn't go prowling for a new relationship, as I was sure I'd never love someone again. Not only because I didn't think there'd be room in my heart, but because the pain of losing someone you love burns so intensely, I didn't think I'd survive if it should ever happen again. But I will tell you a secret – every single bit of pain I have experienced is worth even the tiniest fragment of love I got to have with Andrew. The grief is just powerful, unyielding love left over.

The fact is the all-consuming monster that is grief can and does co-exist with new love. Your heart does not have a finite amount of love to give. It's not America in the middle of a pandemic PPE shortage. It's like when parents go from one child to two - 'how can I possibly love another child as much as my first?'. You can, and you do (...in most cases). The love is not eclipsed, but simply expanded.

My relationship and love with Andrew cannot be replicated, and I don't expect it to be. Matt said to me early on in our friendship, when you're ready to open yourself up again, that person will have to understand what you've gone through and understand the emotions that come along with loss. In my roughest moments, he just understands. *He gets it.* He provides support that I truly think Andrew arranged for KG and me. I don't know what I believe, but I do believe Andrew knew what we needed, and he guided me to it.

Falling in love with Matthew was unconscious in every aspect. I was simply surrounded by his supportive, loving energy while I was shrouded in sweatpants and unkempt hair, and that turned into my heart expanding to include another person. There were mounds of shit all over my life, and he willingly picked up a shovel. And there's a balance that has been struck with respect, caring and kindness to not only myself and KG, but to Andrew.

When I was ready to finally share our relationship with others, I steadied myself to be met with criticism. How can you move on so quickly? I had asked myself the same thing over and over, so I expected some form of it from outsiders. One person on the outer perimeter of my life told me, "This is ridiculous. I'm team Andrew". It was laughable. I'm Team Andrew, too, I say to myself as I walk by his urn every morning.

It's not moral or fair to judge how people manage to handle the end of their world. It's easy to criticize with your very much alive spouse and family at the dinner table. Our life before he died was over. Our plan - mine and Andrew's - was to be married forever. To get KG off to college so that we could go wild in Hawaii, and he could continue asking for a motorcycle and I'd tell him no, it's too dangerous. Those plans changed without any input from me. Life grabs you by the wrist and directs you where to go, says Green Day.

I would hear that I was young, I would find love again. It was dismissive of my pain. As if to say, 'don't worry, one day you'll forget you spent ten years with your wonderful husband'. When I did find love again, it indicated to others that my grief was magically cured and over. "Hooray! She will shut up now!" Love and pain, just like every other emotion we experience as humans, do not exist in a vacuum. Rather, they exist in a blender.

I am allowed to feel and exist and love inside a life I didn't ask or plan for. I'm allowed to find a meaning in the rubble of what is left behind. I'm giving myself permission to let go of what I once felt - the need to make sure everyone around me was comfortable with the space I was taking up in the world - and not give a single uptown funk about opinions that ultimately have no bearing on my or KG's life. This life is tough enough, I don't need to add to it.

I stared through teary eyes at the medium across from me, reading my pain like a book.

"Andrew is ok. You're going to be ok," I nod my head. "He says he'll be seeing you."

My mom and Kris are sitting in the corner, wide eyed in terror as I walk back to them, a sweaty mess. "What did she say to you?"

"Andrew is ok. But he's the one messing with the electricity."

EIGHTEEN
Season of Grief

Grief is not a season.

It's not something to move through, finish, or complete. Not something to pack away like a worn winter coat in the spring. It's not a menu, to which we pick and choose.

It's chaotic and lonesome. Constantly on the brink of the here and the hereafter.

It's all encompassing and it's impatient. It doesn't wait for conveniences. It's menacing, demanding, and inconsiderate.

Grief is guilt. The reminder of every moment wasted, and every sour phrase uttered. A forever aftertaste of bitter words that left your tongue - ones that can never be exchanged for 'I love you' or 'I'm sorry'.

It's a splinter of glass in the palm of your hand, eternally aware of its presence. It's quiet and dull - an unrelenting ache that always occurs in the background. It's a stabbing pain of sorrow when you least expect. A bullet piercing your stomach, your head, your heart.

It is isolating. It's every cliche I've ever read or wrote. It's the broken bits in every bend. It's the 'almost' and the 'not quite'. It's the 'I should have' and 'if only'.

Grief is quiet. An inaudible white noise whispering in silence. It's a symphony of draining emotions. It's loud, ferocious, and aggravating. It is melancholy that reverberates through everything done - the good, the bad and the empty.

It is love. Burgeoning and blooming in perpetuity. A smile, a memory, a moment that echoes in your mind and heart until you physically must react to it. To laugh, to smile, and to cry.

It is every hello and goodbye, all at once, forever, and ever until our last breath.

NINETEEN

A Very Stafford Christmas

What is important to know about grief, for those who are newly initiated or unfamiliar, is that the holidays are wildly painful. As if daily reminders of your person's absence aren't bad enough, we throw a wreathe on it and make it extra festive. We see people with their living, breathing family and think, how has God forgotten us?

The first holiday that was going to wreck my soul after Andrew died was Christmas. It was his favorite holiday. The first year we moved in together, I arrived home from work on Halloween to him putting up our artificial tree.

"Kids aren't even trick or treating yet," I motioned outside, staring at the pumpkins we had yet to carve sitting next to a Christmas stocking.

"Yeah, but it has to be up and ready to light up at midnight," He answered, as if I was the weird one.

Every year after that, we began our own '55 Days of Holiday Cheer' where we'd scour for the best Christmas ornaments and simply enjoy the ambiance of the season. We'd drive around at night delivering vicious critiques of people's Christmas light displays, discussing how we would do it bigger, better, and less (or perhaps more) gaudy if only we had the money. We turned Christmas into a lifestyle, and once we had KG? It was like pouring reindeer pee gasoline on a yuletide fire. We were all in.

We had meetings about what our Christmas wrapping paper theme would be and what kind of holiday activities we could pack in our agenda. He'd drink eggnog by the gallon, dipping Christmas sugar cookies in it like the little holiday elf he was born to be.

The first Christmas without Andrew was going to hurt. The holiday felt like having chicken pox. I'm uncomfortable and feel like hell, and every time I see something that reminds me of Andrew, it's like a nagging terrible itch I shouldn't scratch. I don't want to be around anyone lest my lesions of negativity are contagious and rub off on them. To add salt to our wounds, New Year's Day was our last lost baby's due date. I felt like Scrooge – the Jim Carrey animated version at that. Crawling into an old Victorian bed and being visited by ghosts of Christmas past didn't sound like a bad night for me, but there was a pandemic to work through as a nurse. I was left as a single parent, solely responsible for KG and all of the dogs we had accumulated.

"Are you free on Tuesday evening?" My friend Angie texted me one particularly rough day.

"If I have to go anywhere, then no I'm not," I said half-jokingly. It was during this time I still couldn't manage to be in public or around other people for any length of time without getting overly emotional. People only allow you so many times to spontaneously cry so hard you give yourself a nosebleed in public before they begin to grimace when they see you'll be attending an event.

"Lucky for you it's a zoom thing," Music to my ears. If there was one silver lining to the pandemic, it was the widespread use of zoom taking the place of having to see people in public. And of course, the option for the DoorDash driver to leave the food at your door without having to answer.

I thought maybe Angie had arranged for a meeting with our friends I hadn't spoken to in a while. We'd have a little holiday check in, and then go about our night. I could stay in my two-day old pajamas, it was perfect.

"You're going to get some mail, but don't open it until the zoom," She was stern. Angie was my age but is lovingly authoritative in our interactions. When she spoke, people listened.

Tuesday arrived. A box sat untouched on the counter. If I had to put money on it, I would have bet it was a blanket with Andrew's picture on it. We now had a collection of blankets and pillows with his picture people sent to us. KG and I would put them all on my bed and curl up underneath them.

"If he is looking at us right now, he probably thinks it's funny that his face is all over our bed," KG would laugh.

"I got called into work today, but you're going to get on this zoom at seven tonight with KG, and I'm going to call you later. Love you guys," Angie texted.

Around seven, my mom showed up teary eyed. "Are you ready for the zoom?"

"Ahh…Why are you crying?" I wanted to ask. And what is the big deal with this zoom call? I texted Angie, no response.

I log on and am greeted by two people I recognize but cannot place. These aren't my friends because they're not looking disheveled, and no one is zooming from the bathroom.

"Hi Danielle," they say. They know me, but I'm not sure who they are. Did I have a stroke? A man and a woman sit next to each other, my brain still racing to place who they are. The woman is a beautiful blonde with a megawatt smile.

Oh my god. It clicks. I'm on a zoom with Matthew and Kelly Stafford. At the time, Matthew Stafford was the quarterback for the legendary Detroit Lions. Andrew's team. He would die if he were here right now. If he weren't dead already, that is.

Why am I on a zoom with Matthew Stafford? My ears start ringing and my instant reaction is to do what I do best, and that is to cry. The only other brush with greatness I had ever enjoyed was running into Darko Milicic in a Sharper Image store after the Detroit Pistons won the NBA championship in 2004, but he didn't bother to know my name.

Matthew and Kelly explained that Angie had written to them about our doozy of a year, and they had sent us a package for Christmas. I opened the box and collapsed. My mom, still crying, picked me up by my nervous sweaty arms and stood me back up. They sent us autographed jerseys and a generous check for Christmas gifts for KG. I keep trying to imagine what Andrew would have done. Probably stunned silence I'm sure because he was stoic in nature, but he would have had a perpetual smile for eternity. This would have been the highlight reel of his life. Right up there with KG being born, us getting married, and the time we accidentally stumbled upon a

PlayStation 4 when no one could find them. It is the kind of grandiose, surreal moment you don't ever expect to happen to you.

After getting off the zoom and recovering my heartbeat to a normal rhythm, I scrolled through social media to see that they bless many families each year. Two people who don't have to do anything for anyone, and here they were changing people's lives. It wasn't for the press. It was because of their good hearts. More than anything that night, it felt like Andrew was not forgotten. People must get on with their lives. When you lose someone, it feels like they get further and further away from you as people stop saying their name and sharing stories about them. On that zoom, sitting across from the Stafford's, it felt like he was there with us. His spirit, energy, whatever it is, felt closer than it had in a very long time. How do you thank someone for giving you that moment?

Grief makes you angry. It can make you envious, callous, and miserable. It also makes you grateful. Grateful for the love that feels so far out of your reach, but it shows up at your door or in this case, computer screen. When you are in the deepest, dark pit of despair, people will come to shine a light on you and breathe hope back into your heart. You just have to let them.

TWENTY

Writing

Writing feels like finding a video you yourself find funny and making someone else watch it. You stare at them awkwardly, waiting for their reaction. How embarrassing, am I right? But if we didn't take the leap and force ourselves to share those videos, then the kid who loves corn on TikTok would have never gone viral ("It's corn! I can tell you all about it!"). What's more embarrassing is never trying to chase your dream or in my case, finish writing a book.

My deeply rooted fear of being inadequate was pushed aside in an out of character attempt to share my writing and connect with others. I began telling everyone with ears about this book. It felt awkward and uncomfortable to divulge such information about myself. Sure, I had written through my grief, but who was I to think I had written anything of consequence? Something good enough to be consumed by the public? If I was going to have some skin in the game, I needed to put pressure on myself. There's no greater pressure than letting everyone around you know you were creating something like Frankenstein's monster and letting their expectations hold you accountable. It's sink or swim, boys.

I started writing both physically and purposefully in the mid '90s. Clinton was president. The Bosnia crisis was occurring, and Beanie Babies had the Midwest in an absolute stranglehold. What deeply moved me to write at the time was my dinner.

"I had hot dogs tonight," I wrote with a scribble of enthusiasm. Seven years old and still unable to spell to save a life, but I felt inspired enough to put this thought to paper so that 30 years later I could remember the sentiment. I began to journal every pitiful, immature thought that crossed my mind.

The grand purpose in all of this is the need in me to write - even the most mundane and trivial of life's observations - is as natural as gasping for air when coming up from underwater. Good or bad, the words hang there like clothes drying on a line. What to do with them? Mildew in the heat or get off my ass and put them where they belong.

With Andrew dying, I read a hundred books on the topic of grief. I began to unpack my life and myself because everything was rearranging. I needed to better understand who I was, what grief looks like to others, and how I could learn to function in this cesspool of sadness I was drowning in. I learned everything I could about religious practices related to death and dying. I read the Bible cover to cover. Nothing captured what I was feeling, and I just needed reassurance that what I was feeling was normal or at the very least, legal. Was anyone else suffering, not just from grief, but from the effects of life in general?

Words are my religion. I pray at the altar of their sanctity, and I hope they'll deliver me the divine salvation I search for. After all, it will be words that are left in the rubble of you and I: proof our thoughts and emotions ever existed. Here's hoping aliens can decipher my poor grasp on the English language.

30 years of writing I'm unpacking. Most of it is, *"I had hot dogs for dinner"*. But some bits of it seem like they could offer some guidance to whichever bewildered soul climbs into widowhood or anxious, forlorn adulthood behind me. Who stands stunned into stupor as the chaos of life swirls around them as they try to make sense of it. That is what life is all about, isn't it? Trudging along a course and offering a hand to those behind us. Helping one another see the comedy in the mundane and the beauty in the wreckage of everyday life.

I don't want to be defined by loss. Widow at 33 is such a garbage title. I don't like telling new people that Andrew is gone, but it comes out like vomit. If I seem like a sad sack with no light behind my eyes, it's because I've laid my head on my dead husband's chest and waited for him to take a breath – to tell me it was all a misunderstanding. A medical miracle. A YouTube prank, and now we have ad sponsorships and can quit our day jobs.

I don't doubt other people experience pain and feel emotions intensely, but I just wonder if there's a miswiring in my brain or heart that makes me feel things in an overboard kind of way? Maybe it's mental illness, maybe it's my moon in Virgo. Shoulder shrug. In any event, there has been no therapy, no medication, no physical activity that has given me the healing I need more than writing through life. I read, I write, I repeat.

My husband is dead. Dead, dead, dead – it doesn't even seem like a word anymore. I've tossed it around so much and it's fallen out of my mouth so many times it has taken on a life of its own. A life Andrew should be living, but here we are. My dark humor on paper and his ashes in my foyer, a winning pair.

Everyone has a story waiting to be told, to be written. The feeling of connection keeps us thriving. What is interesting to me is how I cope and if others feel the same way. Surely others on this doomed planet share my brand of neuroticism, and we can rot together in the uncomfortable space that exists in life and loss.

Love, pain, and words bring us together. I choose to believe that now. Otherwise, I'm echoing into the void. My Lexapro prescription and therapist Mary would prefer I stay on the bright side of life.

TWENTY-ONE

Widow Perks

I know this will be surprising to hear, but there are very few perks to your spouse dying. Not what you'd expect, right? There is one positive though, especially if you are a passive people pleaser. It is cancelling services and subscriptions.

A lawn company who I didn't want to waste money on anymore would not let me cancel. I called several times to end things between us, but they had an ironclad grip on me. I would call them fully committed to breaking up and moving on, 'it's not you it's me', but by the end of the chat, they would sweet talk me into adding more services.

A few months after Andrew died, I had no choice but to buck up and not take no for an answer. I gave myself a pep talk. "They won't get you today. You are (mostly) an adult. I believe in you." I'd affirm to myself before pushing the call button.

"...but for only $40 more than what you're paying quarterly, you can get your trees and shrubs sprayed. Don't you want your trees taken care of?" The lady on the other end of the line was so polite. I thought of her having to deal with rude customers, and how I didn't want to be one to add to her list.

"I do. You're right," they drove a soft bargain. I thought of the technicians who would be put out of business if I cancelled. Just add the extra service, Danielle. You can work more next week to pay for it.

"I do care about my trees, very deeply in fact," I start to say.

"As you should. Only good people care about the environment." I shook my head in agreement. My need to be liked was a wet dream to customer service representatives. They didn't have to try too hard; I just wanted them to be impressed by my need to take care of my lawn and my expression of gratitude for all their hard work.

"But the thing is, my husband just died, and I can't afford this anymore." I blurted out.

"Oh my, I am so sorry for your loss. I can discount your final service and cancel our contract expeditiously," she said with a quickness that startled me.

I audibly gasped. That worked? This entire time, I just had to have a dead spouse to cancel lawn care. Do other people know about this loophole?

Maybe she could tell from my voice that I was one of those people who would cry at the drop of a hat, and she needed to quickly close my account and get me off the phone before I emotionally projected onto her. Or maybe she genuinely felt bad. Either way, the account was closed and for the first time in my adult life, I had not allowed my perpetual guilt of being alive to force me to do something I didn't want to do.

"I'd love to keep my cable, but my husband passed away, so I just want the internet now," I became efficient at the whole thing, which was great because there are so many things to take care of when your person dies. Estates, bank accounts, mortgages – it's all a heap of shit you didn't ask to shovel, dumped right on top of your already soiled life. A Disney vacation you had planned and needed refunded immediately because you needed the money to cremate your husband? No problem. Drop the bomb, secure the bag, and keep it moving.

The most satisfying event though is when someone is exceptionally rude to me, and at any other moment in my life, I'd have taken it. But on the other side, Andrew gives me the strength and carte blanche to make them uncomfortable and maybe be a little deadpan snarky back.

I recently replaced my windshield, and the place insisted I do it at my home. "Ma'am I'm telling you; we need to come to you. We just need your garage," he sighed with annoyance.

"That works, but most of my garage is filled with my husband's stuff. I'm not sure there is room."

"Well lady be a better housekeeper or tell your husband to clean up his stuff," he huffed. It was a knife in the heart.

"I would, but he is dead. It's hard to clean the garage when you're dead," The line was silent for a moment.

"I'm sorry," he murmured.

"Yeah, thanks. I'll just take the car elsewhere." He probably went about his day without a second thought, but I would hope he reflected on the conversation and was less abrasive with the next person he spoke to.

In my sick mind, I feel like I'm doing some vigilante justice. Like I'm Batman enforcing politeness on the wicked people of the world who refuse to be a decent person. Maybe sticking your foot in your mouth will make you think twice before you act like the dickhead mayor of Windshield Town, USA.

That's not to say I'm not an absolute bonehead at times. I make a lot of self-deprecating jokes (see: everything in this book), and sometimes it triggers other people. I try to be mindful of who my audience is because my intent is never to laugh or make light at someone else's expense. But would it hurt society if we all maybe gave other people a second thought?

I see flags proudly declaring "fuck your feelings" and ask myself, why? What about other people having emotions is so harmful or threatening to others? This isn't a political ideology argument, but a humanistic one. I ask that in earnest because as an empath, or codependent Virgo take your pick, I have no concept of the need to not care about other people and how they are faring. I don't pretend to have any answers. I barely can get from one day to the next within the confines of my own crazy life, but there has to be some nice, middle ground on the spectrum of 'fuck your feelings' and the "dump your feelings on me, stranger on the street, because I am highly invested" plane I operate on.

Either way, Andrew's death forced me to reflect on myself and my relationship to others. I can't be a rude vigilante. It goes against every fiber of my being, and then I'd go home and dwell on how sad the whole interaction made me. On the flip side, I also can't care about everyone all the time either. It's an impossible task for anyone other than our lord and savior, Dolly Parton.

TWENTY-TWO

Trash Sandwich

I'd say my issues with eating began when a robust woman of 60 fished a cheese sandwich out of a trash can and made me eat it in front of my first-grade peers.

Ms. Lou was a Roald Dahl character who jumped off the page and right into my lunchroom. She towered over the first-grade students, both in stature and in strength. Her credo was 'don't tread on me' and by 'me', she meant the sacred area she occupied in the elementary school cafeteria. The day she caught me discarding a cheese and mustard sandwich, one which I had quickly grown disgusted by, she was out for blood.

"Whose is this??" She stalked up and down the folding table in the lunchroom that smelled of heavily processed meats and elementary fear. A zip lock bag splattered with mustard twisted in her iron grip.

My friends who sat around me were in stunned silence, but I knew if I didn't speak up, they'd be forced to give me up to her.

"It's mine," Immediate tears.

As someone whose instant reflex is to cry, I am not ashamed to break out a few tears every now and then in a social setting. But as an adolescent who was inescapably afraid of getting into trouble, and trying to maintain a reputation of bravery, this was the kiss of death. I would forever be remembered as the kid who threw their entire cheese sandwich away, only to be forced to eat it from the trash can while sobbing like a baby.

Until that day, I had taken great pains to conceal the sandwich in a napkin and force it to the middle section of the trash as to not cause a scene. I was flippant this day, casually tossing it into the can naively thinking I would avoid being reprimanded. Not only did I eat the trash tainted sandwich, I had to "sit on the wall" at recess.

For a quiet child who deathly feared trouble, I found myself sitting on the wall a lot. No adult stopped to consider that children possessed feelings and emotions in the '90s. We were mechanical little monsters who went to school to barely grasp long division and keep big feelings tucked away until we could get home or find nearest bathroom.

I grew up and carried that conflicted relationship with food. When I was in high school, a well-meaning but dimly witted football player asked me, "what happened to you this summer? You used to be skinny".

I wish I could go back and shake some life experience into myself, but body dysmorphia and our societal standards for women forced me to become bulimic. It was at the time 'heroin chic' was the inspiration. Thinness was a personality trait – it was pervasive, and I was lacking the discipline it took to obtain whatever it was I perceived I was inherently devoid of. The punishment for throwing away a cheese sandwich was nothing compared to how my own brain punished myself for eating over 1000 calories.

In college it only got worse. It was the dawn of social media, and this made objectifying yourself much easier. This concept is nothing new. You ask almost any girl or woman, and they can tell you about their own insecure struggle with self-image and weight. Not everyone has their own Ms. Lou, but I'll bet the bank they most certainly have someone in their life who has made a negative comment on their body that has stuck with them through time.

When Andrew died, I couldn't eat for days. After a few weeks, the hunger pain dissipated completely and I figured I'm in for a penny, in for a pound at this point better just see it through and starve myself out. At the very least, I'll leave behind a thin corpse. Dig out the size four jeans from twenty years ago that are stashed in the back of my closet in hopes of a skinny rainy day and bury me in them with the tag sticking out.

"Such a shame," people would say, "Especially now that she is at her ideal weight."

It was such a petty thing to think about, I lamented. Being stuck inside during the pandemic, grieving the loss of my husband, I had nothing to do but examine every single malignant thought that occupied my mind. Why did I ever care what I weighed or how I looked? What did it matter now? Being thin wouldn't bring Andrew back. Our bodies were mere sacks of meat transporting our consciousness from one place to another until The Great Perhaps calls us home.

Two years after Andrew died, I was deep into therapy and Matthew was a part of my life. I recognized that my clothes were a bit snugger, and I referred to it as 'happy love weight'. It occurred to me that I hadn't stepped on a scale in months. Where did that obsessive thought go?

"I think I replaced it with cleaning," I admitted to therapist Mary one session.

"That is one possibility. Do you think you have a different frame of mind?" She was always asking questions I knew she had the answer to.

"…Yes?" I wasn't sure. Everything I thought seemed convoluted. "I guess I just want to be healthy. I want to be here for a while." She shook her head affirmatively and set her pen down.

"Yes Danielle. We want you here for a while. I'll see you next week."

Disordered eating and body image issues don't magically cure themselves. It's a lifelong battle within your own mind and body. When I'm feeling obsessive about food, I take myself back to the moment I brought home Andrew's urn. I wasn't sure what to expect - how much ash or cremains does a body leave behind? I picked him up from the funeral home and carried his white marble urn out of the building in a reusable grocery bag. It was heavier than I expected. I laced my arm around the bottom, squeezing it to my chest to make sure it didn't fall.

"If I drop you, you're going to be so pissed," I said aloud in the parking lot, feeling his soul walking next to me with his arm outstretched to make sure I made it to the car in one piece.

"This is all we will be in the end," I got into the passenger seat, Andrew's urn in my lap and closed the door. Kris and my mom stared at it somberly. We sat silently and cried.

Every now and then, I walk by his urn and pick it up to give me a reminder of what is important. And to pull a 'gotcha' on Andrew's ghost, pretending I'm going to drop it.

TWENTY-THREE

Quiet Quitting

Every morning post Andrew's death, I'd start my workday by waking up every fifteen minutes checking the clock beginning at midnight. Finally, I'd roll out of bed for my first of several panic attacks of the day. My body would get increasingly stiff and uncomfortable. My jaw would chatter, and my neck ached. I'd cry a bit, give myself a pep talk, and move on to the next task of getting to work. I'd drive the ten minutes to the hospital, listening to Bulls of Parade by Rage Against the Machine at the loudest volume to drown out my crying. Beginning to wind down, I'd take a couple of deep breaths and try another approach to get myself in the door – positive self-talk.

Nothing really helped. Part of the struggle was being a nurse during an unprecedented pandemic, but most of it was Andrew's death. The last place I was before my world collapsed was in that building, taking care of other people's loved ones when Andrew was wheeled into the emergency department twenty miles away. I'll sometimes look at the floor in the hospital where I work, and I'll think of the trauma bay where he died. And then I'll see his face.

I pulled his hand out from underneath the blankets. His body was already pulled onto a body bag. His fingertips dirty with grease, from whatever last thing he was doing. His eye was still half open, void, and lifeless. What was the last thing he saw? The ugly signs of death that already started to take over and take him from us colored the back of his body. I think of driving home from his work in his car and gripping onto some random rag that was thrown on his floor. I felt like if I could just wring my hands bloody with that rag in my hand, maybe he'd walk through the door. Maybe it'll all be a nightmare. Maybe our daughter could crawl into his lap and laugh that he was being mean for playing a trick on us. Maybe...

And that's all just from glancing at the hospital floor.

My coworkers who helped try to breathe life back into me didn't know how to deal with whatever shell of a human was left of me. Either they avoided me entirely or wondered why I was so off. Both served as reminders that everything was different in my world. I'd listen to everyone call their significant others at the end of the day, deciding what's for dinner or saying they loved them, and they'd see them soon. If the windows weren't sealed shut, I would have jumped out of them.

"Where have you been?" My favorite maintenance worker asked a few weeks after I had returned to work.

"Ah, I just took some time off," I bit my tongue to try and keep the words to myself, but they forced themselves out through my teeth. "My husband died."

"Oh man, I'm sorry to hear that. That's a bummer," he shook his head and tapped my shoulder with condolences. He began to joke about something, but I tuned it out. A bummer. I couldn't make out if he was uncomfortable and wanted to change the subject, or if he was simply nonchalant about death, but it was a knife in the heart. I had to file someone else under "favorite maintenance worker" after that day.

My boss was sympathetic and understanding to my flightiness and deeply broken heart. The trouble with being a boss is that after a while, it doesn't matter if a heart is broken – work still must be done. You must get back to life, I'd keep telling myself. But does getting back to life mean I have to have a severe panic attack several times a week, and sit in a parking lot screaming and crying lyrics to Rage Against the Machine?

The final straw was when the thought of work made me want to kill myself. I thought I'd rather drive off the road and die than walk into that building one more time. So, I quit. Our society doesn't leave too much space for us to process emotions. Bereavement time off for an immediate family member was three days. Three days. That was just enough time to plan what to do with his body. It felt wrong to quit a perfectly good job. One I fiercely loved before he died with the best coworkers, but I couldn't put myself through the trauma of reliving that day anymore. I needed to give myself time and space to heal.

I spent a few months getting my sleep schedule on track and going to therapy which I should have sought out years before. But because mental health and wellness isn't as accessible in America as say, Taco Bell, I found other means to cope. Mary, my therapist, was an older lady who was very soft spoken and had a flair for interior design. Her office was the library of my dreams, and she always had a tissue up her sleeve. She reminded me of an American Maggie Smith in the movie Sister Act, but less nun-ish. Having never been to a therapist before, it surprised me that she kept a pad of paper in her lap and occasionally wrote notes during our sessions. I guess the movies got some things right.

"I hope I'm getting a good grade," I laughed, half-joking and half-serious.

She smiled warmly. "That's something else we have to work on." Oh. She has a running list of shit that is wrong with me. Hopefully it's all a DSM-5 diagnosable disorder that has a treatment algorithm.

"I guess I just need to know if I'm doing this right?" I questioned, slightly leaning over to see if I could see her list of what was wrong with me.

"If you're doing grief right?"

"If I'm doing life right," I thought for a moment. Andrew dying and our lives imploding meant I had to completely restructure my life and myself. Who am I in this new life?

"Do you think you are?" she asked, as if I could give her an answer to that loaded question. If we're basing it on age, I am in fact a card-carrying adult. I do adult things like go to work, file taxes, and send thank you cards. But am I performing life right?

Since I can remember I have never truly known who I am. I would glance around at others, living their seemingly authentic lives, and wonder how it was so easy for them to operate? How can you just have opinions and freely express them without fear of rejection or humiliation, I wanted to interview them.

But then, Andrew died. And it was the stark realization that any moment can completely wipe your consciousness off this planet. Will it really matter then what anyone thought of you? The sad part is that you're going to experience humiliation and rejection whether you are yourself or you're someone else, so you might as well live authentically. The walls we put up to keep the bad out keep the good out too. It's all poorly insulated against tragedy - there will always be a draft of bad coming through. It's cliche and easy to read and be told by a therapist. But when you sit down across from your husband's urn and consider the years that were stripped from him, it's now your duty to stop living so scared.

After a few months, I found a new job because a girl must pay her bills. I walked into a building with no one knowing who I was before or that KG and I were up the night before trying on her dead father's hats. I was able to be a nurse again and form new professional relationships. Brick by brick, I began to build a new life. It doesn't happen overnight. It happens in your own time, in little fragments of moments where you exist within your love and loss.

TWENTY-FOUR

Poop Bag

The pandemic was a nightmare for everyone. It had an extra layer of difficulty for those of us in the IBS struggle. "No public restroom" signs posted on doors of gas stations and stores everywhere spelled disaster.

"We're all friends here," our monthly friend brunches slowly took the place of my therapy. "Have you ever had to poop in a trash bag?"

"Poop in a bag at home or in the wild?" Alexis laughed.

"Yes," Kelly answered with absolution. There were no pretenses with this group of people.

"Why would you have to poop in a bag at home?" Jen asked.

"I was leaving the gym and had an emergency, but I couldn't go back into the gym because they were locking up. So, I ran into the grocery store, but that bathroom was closed. I had no options," I admitted as if under oath.

"Fuckin' covid man," Kelly rolled her eyes, taking a sip of her mimosa. She was no stranger to extreme measures.

Once a month we'd gather at our local diner, like a bunch of southeastern Michigan Sex and the City knock offs. That is, if the premise of Sex and the City was more about child rearing and the girls regularly discussed shitting themselves. We would catch up on life, exchanging thoughts on our nursing careers and the possibility of building a women led commune that would operate off the grid. They had witnessed the best and worst of my issues, the latest IBS debacle being one of the worst.

"You couldn't beat this information out of me, and you're just casually sharing it over a farmer's skillet," Jen was disgusted. She didn't have the same tawdry sense of humor and preferred we kept the IBS talk to a minimum at the table.

"Look, I'm not bragging about it because I'm proud. I'm just wondering when this madness will end. We need bathrooms. When I discussed the situation with Mary…"

"I'm sorry, you told your therapist you shit in a bag?" Alexis stopped me.

"It kind of came up. We talk about everything." I side-eyed the group, defending my choice of therapy session material. Maybe I didn't need to talk to her about everything, but I was getting increasingly stressed out worrying what to talk about in therapy. I needed a break from talking about Andrew.

Mary would cycle through notes when a lull in the session would happen, and the silence would make me feel awkward so I'd try to fill it with whatever I could.

"I didn't cry this week," I'd proudly announce, looking for a gold star of approval.

"You didn't cry," she'd repeat back. "Do you consider that a win?" My mind wanders back to the panic attack I suffered in a grocery store a few weeks previous. I had walked by a tuna lunch kit that Andrew always liked and descended into a puddle of tears. Workers gathered around to see what they could do, but there was nothing to be done other than ringing up the 15 tuna kits and getting me out of that store.

"Yeah, I'd say it's a win."

Mary instructed me to sit in my grief, and after I learned what that meant, I had no trouble doing it. The problem was that it was all I wanted to do. I didn't want to laugh or leave the house. The tragic thing is that the turmoil and sadness made me feel closer to Andrew and it's hard to let go of that. If only I am sad enough, he will come back to life. If that were the case, I'd be a world class necromancer.

If I don't let go, I am missing out on what is left of my time here. What a balance to strike. It all boils down to me feeling this: it's just not fair. It's unfair that his life was cut short. Unfair that KG lost her dad. It's unfair that it's always a diarrhea Russian roulette when it comes to eating anything other than soup for me. I suppose life doesn't hinge on fairness though. Otherwise, things like Jack the Ripper, cancer, and the Grammys wouldn't exist.

My friends kept me from self-destructing. They laughed with me back to life again. If not for them, I would probably still be inside my house three years later, unable to move forward. They dragged me back into the world. A covid world, where bathrooms were closed, and I was forced to poop in a bag (much to Jen's chagrin), but I'll take what I can get.

TWENTY-FIVE

She is small. I wonder how that much energy can fit into someone so small. She untucks herself from me, runs off the porch swing and over to her daddy's tree. It's a pink Magnolia. Underneath it is a statue of a weeping angel, her wings large around her. We have no grave, so this is our physical place to mourn - as if it's not everywhere, all the time.

This is her time to talk to him without me around. She's still afraid she'll make me cry. I tell her it's okay to cry. We talk about the things he loved; things that would make her smile and laugh. She likes to hear stories, as if she can close her eyes and exist in the memory.

"I'll be your story keeper, KG," I whisper to her. It's a hard job to have to remember all the time. She's afraid of forgetting, but we talk about him so much, I tell her, "I don't think that's possible."

She shrugs and continues with her day - with the little thoughts which scurry through her head that I'm sure I'm not even fully aware of. She astounds me with her aptitude for emotional intelligence. Does such a loss make someone more empathetic, more sensitive to the energy and emotions around her? She was always that way though, perhaps just heightened now.

I do not know what her struggle is like. I lost my partner, but she lost her daddy. No father daughter dances, no daddy date nights on weekends. No more unicorn necklace and oversized teddy bear surprises from him. There is a hole that cannot be filled.

She comes into my room at night, tears streaming down her face, *"are you sure he's never coming back? Are you sure he's in Heaven? Can I go there?"*

I don't know how to parent through that. I'm doing it and I'm trying my best, but there is no manual. Despite what you may read in every book in the self-help and grief section of Barnes & Noble there is no easy way to help a child recover their innocence. Their innocent belief that everyone lives until they're 90 and life is perfect. Now she's afraid of death at six years old.

She goes to her therapist, and we don't keep our emotions hidden. We invite them for dinner, and we deal with them as we need to. On days like today, I give her space to talk to her Daddy. Sometimes when she's done, we discuss it. Other times she moves along to the next fun thing of the day. She sits at the tree until a butterfly lands on the grass nearby.

"Oh! There you are," she grins. She looks over to me, pointing at the butterfly. "Daddy says hi"

TWENTY-SIX

Never Better

After Andrew died, I didn't know how to interact with the world without being overwhelmingly sad or angry. I was a bull and everything outside of my door was a China shop. Every line of questioning made me want to plead the fifth. Well-meaning inquiries of "how are you doing?" was like a needle being driven into my eyes.

"Do you really want to know?" I'd think to myself. Well, last night I measured to see if my shower rod could support my weight to hang myself. I don't sleep. I can't think straight. My old life is over. Nothing is funny and everything is pointless. It wasn't fair to everyone that I was an angry ball of emotions, so I'd usually muster an answer with a sarcastic "never better" or "living the dream". They'd laugh - either out of relief I was trying to be funny again or out of discomfort of my awkwardness.

Andrew dying burnt off any layer of protection from pain I had, and even the slightest breeze would send me into a fit of misery. What was worse than being confronted with how to answer how I was doing? The silence some people bestowed upon me.

"Altogether disappeared with him. Fuck me I guess," I complained to my mom as we assembled another grief purchase. Bookshelves, kitchen islands, basketball hoops – whatever I could get my hands on.

My mother, not unlike myself, is loyal to a fault. We are blinded to the other side of things when we feel someone we love is hurt. If someone has done us wrong, then it's, "fuck them," which is exactly what she replied. Unscrewing what I incorrectly put together and fixing it without making a fuss, she shook her head. She had spent the first few months of the pandemic stuck dealing with my labile mood and rehashing the same thing repeatedly.

Death, grief, and mental health crisis make most people uncomfortable, and quite understandably so. There's no handbook on how to deal with it, but from my personal experience, silence echoes louder than any poor choice of words ever could. What you don't know is silence and avoidance feel like dying all over again.

I sat at home surrounded by people the day after Andrew died, and I kept repeating "I'm alone, I'm alone and you'll all leave". They thought I was in shock, but I knew what I was in for. They'd all get to leave and go on with their lives, but KG and I would still be here. Stuck in a goddamn nightmare with nothing but his clothes and pictures and everything left over to remind us of his absence. People seemingly forgot that the last piece of Andrew, his daughter, was now left without a dad and a grieving, pitiful mother.

If we're being honest, dying doesn't scare me. After Andrew, it seemed like a welcome relief from the pain I was living. What scared me was thinking of my family dealing with the aftermath. The messes they'd have to clean up, the financial burden it would place on them. But most of all, my sweet KG being an orphan – the mere thought was enough to right myself. It only took a split second of thinking of her to make me back my car away from the river I considered driving into. I'd say grief makes you crazy, but in my case – it makes you even crazier.

"Well," I sighed as if to make an announcement at one of our monthly brunches. "I think I'm finally doing better."

Kelly watched in disgust as I sloppily ate the olives out of my bloody Mary. A few minutes before while ordering, I asked for French toast and potatoes.

"Okay carb girl," the server rolled her eyes at my unabashed gluttony and snatched the menu from me before I could order more.

"Are you better because of all the carbs?" Kelly lost her mother in her early twenties. She watched cancer take her away, so I considered her a bit of a grief mentor for myself.

"The pain doesn't go away. It becomes different. You learn to live with it," she'd reassure me. "You don't have to be better for anyone else. You need to be gentle with yourself."

It was Kelly who made me cry at work a few weeks before Andrew died. We were caring for a hospice patient, when the family left the room to take a break and get lunch. We gently cleaned the patient up and repositioned her to be more comfortable. I watched as Kelly gingerly combed her hair and spoke to her in soft, lullaby whispers. The patient wasn't responsive, but it didn't matter. Kelly gave the patient her all, the empathy pouring out of her.

We walked out of the room, and I burst into tears. As nurses, we were well accustomed with death, so it was unusual for me to react that way. But it was watching the act of empathic caring Kelly gave that moved me.

"She reminds me of my mom," she admitted.

"I'd want you to take care of my family," I hugged her. It's the sincerest flattery you can give to another nurse, to trust them with your own kin.

We moved on – more patients to see, a cheeseburger in the cafeteria to devour.

Two years later I'd find myself in the same hospital. This time not as a nurse, but as a patient. I had been having increasingly crushing chest pain and trouble breathing. I was sweaty and anxious and thought, "well, this is it." For good measure WebMD confirmed, "you're dying. Get your affairs in order". No need for the shower rod or the river – my broken heart was going to be the thing to take me out at 35 years old.

I trampled into the emergency room, clutching my chest trying not to panic even more than I already was. "I'm either having a heart attack or some really embarrassing gas," I chuckled.

They did their usual workup of EKG and blood work, and I considered maybe I should post a vague picture of my IV on Instagram to garner a little interest in my health dilemma. Because I sat in the room for a while and wasn't enjoying a groin shaving for a stent placement, I deduced it was probably an embarrassing anxiety attack.

I breathed a sigh of relief as my chest pain subsided, and I glanced at the monitors as my vital signs trended down to normal. "Just an expensive panic episode," I said to no one, but in my defense, the worst one I had ever experienced. I checked the date. It was a few days before the anniversary of Andrew's death. No wonder my heart was screaming.

"Good news," the doctor barged into the room without a hint of enthusiasm. "You're ok, your heart is fine. May want to consider weight management though," casually regarding me the same way the carb girl server had. "How do you feel?"

I thought the question over. Andrew was dead. Death was a part of life, and I had to learn to deal with it. I had to start over, parent alone, snake the shower drain by myself. I had to change my emergency contact and wipe him off all our accounts – like the accident wiped him off this earth. I'm angry, depressed and confused, and overweight apparently. But it's not a heart attack. I'm ok. KG is ok. My teeth are finally at a good place and almost straight. I'm going to get my ducks back in order until the next earthquake comes to disrupt our lives, but until then, we're going to live well. There's no finish line of grief. There's love, there's loss, and then there's life on the other side of that. How do I feel?

"Never better."

Final Thoughts

My favorite thing about staying home from school in the '90s was watching The Jerry Springer Show. At the end, he'd share his final thoughts, and bring the camera in close to tell us "Take care of yourself...and each other". It felt like such a neat little bow to wrap up an episode full of violent homophobia and outrageous paternity fights.

Now that you know more about me than you probably bargained for, I'm going to pull you in for my final thoughts. I have no advice to offer. If you haven't inferred by my egregious use of curse words and stories about shit, I am an expert in nothing. I am just as lost as you are. What I can say is that it took 33 years and my husband dying for me to realize how fragile life truly is. We don't only live it in the big moments. It's also in the tiny, seemingly inconsequential moments of our daily lives.

Because our death is such an anonymous expiration date, we must be vigilant in living and loving completely. Take your leap. Live your life. Reach out and connect before we're ashes. Swallow down any insecurity that keeps you from pursuing the life you want for yourself. It's not easy, but neither is watching someone die with regret. As Andrew's death has proven to me, we are not guaranteed any last words. Say 'I love you' even if it's for the millionth time – even if you're angry. Take the picture - even if you're having a bad hair day. And above all else dear friends, don't forget to return your cart to the cart corral.

I'll be seeing you. xx

Acknowledgements

KG - you're the greatest gift life has offered me, and I would never re-gift you. Thank you for being my reason. Thank you for always flushing when you go to the bathroom. You amaze me every day. Whoever you become, you are the absolute best person I've ever known, and I love you to the furthest reaches of ever-expanding space.

America's Best Dance Crew aka my mom, dad, and sister Kris. Thank you for keeping me together when I couldn't do it myself. For cleaning out my yard and building all the furniture I grief ordered during the pandemic. For letting me take depression naps. For waking me up from depression naps. Your love has been a warm blanket.

Matthew, you're a blessing. If there was a love lottery, I would be the grand prize winner. If this is a simulation, then whoever is playing my character is using cheat codes to get me the absolute best partner. You are all my good days, and I hope I'm yours too. ILY.

My emotional support persons: Kelly, Alexis, Jen, Maddie. You were there for me when I wasn't even there for myself. The world would be a better place if everyone had friends like you. Thank you for being the Pokémon evolution of fun coworkers, to hilarious best friends, to your final form - my family.

I must give flowers to the best neighbors in the biz – Shelly, Dan, Dale, Peggy, Janet & the boys. Thank you for being there for me when Andrew died and teaching me how to efficiently rake up leaves. Thanks for never calling the cops on our idiot dogs.

The folks in my life who show up for me in ways that they probably don't even realize: Kim, Aimee, Hollie, Amanda, Nicole, Jeremy, Aunt Steph, Cathy, Loretta, Judy. And of course, those who put up with me as a young adult & will be featured protagonists in future essays of mine: Gina, Jen, Phyllis, Jenny Penny, Bridget, Jessica.

Matthew and Kelly Stafford are absolute angels. Detroit misses you.

And finally, because you're not here to complain about being last, to Andrew. For being my partner in a life I didn't expect to ever live or feel I deserve. For not breaking up with me when I had a very dramatic mental breakdown when I cut my hair off in 2010. We miss you every second of our days. I hope wherever you are, it is beautiful.

About the Author

Danielle is a writer, widow, & an overly observant mess with tattoos that probably will not age well. She resides in Michigan with her daughter KG and multiple dogs. Follow her on Instagram @ danielleoubeck.